This Rabbit is Constipated!

Reports from the front row at Slimbridge
Dowsing Group – mostly by Trish Mills
As seen in the local Gazette

Quicksilver Publications

First published by Quicksilver Publications in the United Kingdom 2011 on behalf of Slimbridge Dowsing Group
www.slimbridgedowsers.org.uk

ISBN 978-0-9557600-5-1

All profits to Slimbridge Dowsing Group

Type set in Palatino 12 point
Origination by Patricia J Mills
Printed and bound by Berforts Group Ltd., Stevenage, Herts

Contents

Colour Photographs

Thanks and acknowledgements to photographers
who have contributed photographs over the
years, many of which have appeared in the
Gazette. Notably this includes Patrick Callaghan,
Peter Golding and Peter Gibson.

Foreword

by Peter Golding, Chairman

Whilst proof reading this book and reliving all the interesting activities we have had since 2007, my mind went back to 2003 when about eight people asked me to teach them to dowse, and I invited them to come and receive instruction on my back lawn.

They came regularly every week and were fascinated by the many applications of dowsing, and thrilled that they could get dowsing reactions to the underground pipes and cables around my house. One of the ladies said, "I don't think you will be able to teach me Peter, I am ninety-two years old."

She turned out to be one of the most accurate dowsers – including map dowsing.

After a few weeks, when they felt they had achieved all they wanted, some of them left and others joined these informal gatherings. No fee was charged but any voluntary contributions were placed in a sealed Donation Box.

When numbers increased we moved into the Slimbridge Village Hall and eventually formed the small Slimbridge Dowsing Group with a committee to share the workload. The £80 content of my 'Donation Box' was handed over to the treasurer.

Mainly as a result of the publicity from these articles written by Trish Mills, published in the Dursley *Gazette*, and the excellent presentation of these articles on my website by my webmaster, Simon Olley, the word got round that a 'new' and exciting activity (dowsing is thousands of years old!) was being pursued in Slimbridge. We had visitors from all over Gloucestershire and beyond.

We now hold meetings twice a month, with speakers from across the country as well as our 'home grown', now experienced dowsers, and have enthusiastic members and visitors from the six counties around our village. I believe we must be the most active dowsing group in the country.

This success would probably not have been achieved without the hard work and eye-catching articles written by Trish. Many people are worthy of praise, but most of all I feel that special thanks should be given to her for the publicity she has generated, and I hope this book she has produced will prove to be very popular and she will be rewarded by the demand as it flies off the shelves.

Acknowledgements

Lists of thanks to all and sundry can make for boring reading, but it would be remiss of me not to acknowledge our local newspaper, the *Gazette*, which has faithfully published our reports during the last four years, and thereby made us famous.

Publicity is the oxygen of any organisation, and our numbers have increased accordingly. I must also thank Simon Olley, our wonderful webmaster, who regularly puts our reports on our website.

We must also thank all our amazing and wonderful speakers. In four years we have only had one that I refused to write about!

I hasten to add, I didn't write every single report, as there were occasions when I missed a meeting. So I must thank Barbara Davis, Peter Gibson and Barry Goldring for the occasions they stepped into the breach.

Also sincere thanks to all our Slimbridge Dowsing Group members, who are delightful people, interesting in their own right, who have come along and learned and persevered and supported the Group. It is a remarkable privilege to mix with like-minded people.

And finally, thanks are due to our Chairman, Peter Golding, who started the whole thing in the first place.

Trish Mills

Preface

The Slimbridge Dowsing Group began life in 2003, and Peter Golding frequently sent brief reports of their activities to the Dursley *Gazette*'s Community News pages. Membership grew so that, by November 2006, there were enough people to form a Committee and put things on an official footing. Peter wrote the following for the *Gazette*, and it appeared on 23rd November 2006.

"The Slimbridge Dowsing Group, after three years in existence, has held its formal inaugural meeting to approve a constitution and elect a Committee.

The Group's founder, Peter Golding, was elected Chairman, Peter Gibson, Vice-Chairman; Trish Mills, Secretary; Barry Goldring, Treasurer; with committee members Ann Jones, Brian Davies and Donald Smith.

In his address, Peter Golding outlined the group's remarkable achievements to date. These included the discovery of two local labyrinths, outlines of archaeological features such as Dursley Castle, Slimbridge Chantry Chapel, Gossington monastic buildings and an Iron Age camp near Minsterworth. Members have learnt how to find underground streams and estimate their depth and flow rate.

Remarkable successes have been achieved in 'healing' with the aid of dowsing, in both humans and animals. Recently, a lady in Australia had sent a message of deep gratitude for the successful remote healing her teenage daughter received.

The committee members have agreed a programme of fortnightly activities for the next five months. These include basic dowsing training, exploring earth energies and ley lines, labyrinths and archaeological dowsing exercises.

Membership is open to anyone, whether or not they have any experience of dowsing – we will teach them."

And we have! At the time of going to press in 2011, we have some 40 members, most of whom can dowse.

2007

Before we begin . . .

You are welcome to try this at home – in fact, we hope you will, but before we begin dowsing, we need to prepare ourselves first.

Start by asking, "Please may I dowse? Am I ready to dowse? Should I dowse?" If your dowsing rods move in the 'No' direction to any of these questions, you should wait a while, rest, and drink some water before trying again. You need to centre yourself, and feel calm within. Sometimes it's just not appropriate to dowse at all, the rods will tell you.

Once you've received the OK, you need to protect yourself. At our Dowsing Questioning Skills Forum at the beginning of 2011, our three wise men, Peter Golding, Peter Gibson and Barry Goldring, each revealed their techniques for such protection, which relies on visualisation – usually envisaging a cloak of blue or white light or a shield of shining silver around you.

What ever form it takes, hold on to that image and ask, "Am I protected?" This enables you to avoid any harmful energies when you open your mind to receive the information you seek.

Earth Energies and Leylines with Peter Gibson
Thursday 11th January 2007

Slimbridge Dowsing Group continues to go from strength to strength with an influx of new members already this year. This is no doubt due to an exciting programme, which is open to non-members and non-dowsers too.

At a meeting in Slimbridge Church on 11th January, 16 attendees heard a talk by member Peter Gibson on Earth Energies and Ley Lines. There are many types of energy that can be dowsed on the earth's surface and may come from specific parts of the earth, faults and movements within the earth, or outside from solar, lunar or planetary sources.

Peter described the awareness of earth energies in China, where feng shui involves the balancing of beneficial and detrimental energies to create harmony in both home and business life. Balancing, directing and reinforcing the energies that keep us alive and in good health is used in acupuncture, acupressure and in dowsing for health.

He then showed a drawing of the earth energies he had found on the site of the Iron Age Camp at Churcham near Gloucester, where energy vortexes were found rising from and entering the earth, together with spirals of energy in joined pairs within sacred areas.

Members were then shown how to locate energies rising from underground streams, several of which run under Slimbridge Church. A powerful vortex of energy was discovered in the front of the central aisle.

Outside, the suspected ley line was soon found, being a detectable straight line joining raised points in the landscape where sacred and secular sites exist.

It was found that the Church lies within a broad beam of neutral and balanced energy discernable with dowsing rods, and several spirals were found.

Further dowsing will enable recording of the many energies which centuries of worship have attracted to this wonderful building.

Dowsing for Health with Peter Golding
Saturday 27th January 2007

Dowsing for water, and even for oil, is now well known, but dowsing for health and, more specifically, for allergies, is not so familiar. During his talk in Slimbridge Village Hall on Saturday morning, 27th January, Chairman Peter Golding surprised his audience by demonstrating how simple the procedure can be.

Peter asked a volunteer 'patient' to hold different items of food in turn, such as a bottle of beer, a bar of chocolate, a packet of oats, an orange or a biscuit, and then dowsed to see whether this person was allergic to any of them. The volunteer was delighted to discover she was not allergic to alcohol and to have it confirmed that she was allergic to wheat.

It is even possible to ask specific questions such as whether the allergy is to additives in the food rather than the food itself. The audience laughed when Peter asked how many small beers were good for him, and how many were bad. (Four seemed to be his limit!)

After the demonstration, Peter gave members of the audience the opportunity to dowse themselves for allergies, which can also be done by simply naming the suspect food, and not necessarily holding it. The response given by a dowsing rod or crystal pendulum can frequently be more accurate than a medical blood test.

Peter further demonstrated dowsing for other medical problems, and was able to offer healing too. He told the group about absent healing, which can be done with a photograph, on a sufferer as far away as Australia.

Hands on Healing with John Mayo
Thursday 8th February 2007

Hands-on healing is somewhat different from dowsing, but when international healer John Mayo gave a talk at Slimbridge Dowsing Group on Thursday, 8th February, there was an excellent turnout and attendees were fascinated.

John discovered his unusual healing abilities by accident just twelve years ago when he was 53 years old. His wife had been involved in a serious traffic accident, resulting in headaches and leg pain. In sympathy, John held his wife's head in his hands, and they were both surprised when the headache went away and did not return. She then asked for his healing touch on her legs and John was incredulous when they too seemed to be healed.

Since then, John has healed many people of all ages, races and religions, including animals and even a boa constrictor! It is not necessary to believe in it to be healed – 95% of women do but 95% of men don't!

John has travelled extensively, both in the UK and abroad, administering healing, giving radio interviews and contacting patients by telephone. He has discovered that if listeners put a handkerchief or tissue over the loudspeaker or telephone, and afterwards place it on the afflicted area, they can receive healing that way too.

There were many questions from the audience and John followed up by applying hands-on healing to the leg of one of the dowsers, during which the dowser used his pendulum to detect the healing energy entering his leg from John's left hand and coming out through his right hand.

Water Divining with Peter Golding
Saturday 24th February 2007

In these times of drought, water shortages, hosepipe bans and soaring water bills, the ancient art of water divining is attracting more interest than ever before.

The good turnout for Peter Golding's talk on Saturday, 24th February in Slimbridge Village Hall was encouraging: it included regular members and several visitors who had travelled from as far afield as Kent, Newbury (and Wotton-under-Edge!) to listen and learn.

Water divining skills are becoming ever more sought after and while Peter, our Chairman, is much in demand, he is keen to teach others in order that they too can offer this remarkable service. There is a lot to discover and absorb.

Based on the idea of locating water for a local farmer so that he could sink a borehole on his land and be independent of the water companies, Peter began his talk by demonstrating the types of dowsing rod he uses – L-rods and Double-V rods – and gave a demonstration of how he goes about his search.

Obviously the rods can only answer yes or no, so Peter's questions are couched in such terms as "Is there a source of flowing water more than 50ft down but less than 100ft down?" When the rods indicate yes, the accuracy can be refined by counting – "50ft, 55ft, 60ft . . .?" and continuing until the rods respond again.

More questions are asked in order to establish the direction from which the water is flowing, the gallons-per-minute that can be expected, its mineral content and its drinking quality. Peter always makes a point of thanking his source for the information given, but admits he does not know from whence the answers come.

Once you have established a suitable site on which to sink your borehole, you then have to brief the driller, and provide him with a considerable amount of geological information. We were shown specialised geological maps, 3-D models of rock strata and small samples of a variety of rock, gravel, sand and clay.

"If I find a lot of clay at the site," says Peter, "my heart sinks because clay is impermeable and the likelihood of success is significantly reduced; also, the depth of any water under the clay layer is more difficult to predict."

As always when a talk is particularly interesting, the time passed too quickly and the group went out to the village hall car park to practise their new skills. It is thrilling when the rods respond and most people present met with an encouraging amount of success. They detected a large quantity of excellent quality water deep under the car park and someone joked that they should sink a large borehole immediately.

Labyrinth or Maze? with Peter Golding
Thursday 8th March 2007

The difference between a labyrinth and a maze is an interesting one. In his talk to the Slimbridge Dowsing Group on Thursday 8th March, Chairman Peter Golding explained that you enter a maze in order to get lost; it's part of the fun. Whereas a labyrinth has only one path, so you cannot get lost: you enter to 'find' yourself, to enjoy a spiritual experience of enlightenment and healing in a hallowed place.

Titleing his talk 'A Maze in Troytown', (the name means turf maze), Peter explained that labyrinths are usually ancient and only to be found through dowsing, since the site has probably been ploughed hundreds of times over the years and no visible trace remains.

The labyrinth at Troytown in Longaston Lane, Slimbridge is believed to be 1,500 years old, and may have been used on many occasions since then. Today, dowsers can create their own labyrinth in their back garden and walk it regularly for a calming, uplifting feeling at its centre, for meditation and problem solving.

When asked about size, Peter revealed that labyrinths can be any size, from a small one drawn on a piece of paper and 'walked' with a pencil, to a model or representation such as a plaque on the wall, to the full-size version that can be larger than the Slimbridge village hall in which the meeting took place.

Labyrinths can be made of any material – raised turf, hedges, pebbles or stones. What they all have in common, however, is that at their centre they have a strong concentration of energy and frequently, water is to be found beneath. Most are also crisscrossed with energy lines or ley lines; the one at Troytown is intersected by energy leys going towards a marker stone near Whitehouse Farm on the Old Dursley Road west of the A38, and lines passing either side of Slimbridge church. There is even a rogue energy line that appears to emanate from the centre of the labyrinth itself.

Although it was a wonderful sunny day, the only disappointment for the audience of eighteen was that plans to visit Troytown and dowse the labyrinth for themselves were thwarted by previous days of rain. The field was too sodden and the farmer understandably did not want such a large group trampling mud and young crops. Likewise, a proposed visit to privately-owned land near the canal was not possible, again because it was too wet.

So we remained in the village hall and Peter Gibson, a long-standing member with a special interest in archaeological dowsing, taught us how to map-dowse for labyrinths and spirals instead. Peter Golding also taught us how to draw them (surprisingly complicated) and how to behave when we do visit a real one, hopefully in May.

"It is important", said Peter, "to respect the place you are in, to bow before you enter at the only entrance, frequently north facing, to follow the path to the centre, and to enjoy the privilege of being there. On your return journey, you should reflect on what you have experienced and, as you leave, turn and bow again, or perhaps say Amen in farewell."

Amazing Troytown!

Basic Surveying Techniques with Barry Goldring
Saturday 24th March 2007

There is more to being a dowser than simply dowsing. A dowser seeking water needs to have at least some knowledge of geology and anyone dowsing for health and healing needs some biological information, or at least some very detailed checklists. And an archaeological dowser, using rods or pendulum to discover ancient ruins, needs basic surveying techniques.

Consequently, Barry Goldring's talk on Saturday 24th March drew an interested crowd. Barry is an experienced archaeological dowser, and keen to impress the importance of recording measurements and compass bearings in relation to a prominent feature such as a tree or corner of a field. This enables the dowser to prepare scaled drawings of the dowsed outlines of ancient buildings or other features on the site.

Barry then produced a most impressive scaled drawing he had made of the terraced garden at Woodchester Park, showing contour lines and the outline of archaeological features discovered there by dowsing. He went on to show the various tools he uses for his surveying work, such as marker pegs, labels, flags, measuring tapes, prismatic compass, GPS receiver and the all-important clipboard with rainproof cover.

Members were invited to review the form Barry uses to record information about specific archaeological features. Using his rods, Barry can ask such questions as to what was the primary purpose of the building – church, abbey, castle, etc., which materials had been used in the walls and roof, their diameter, thickness and height, the position of posts, doors and windows, and even the year it was built and when it was last used.

An Introduction to Dowsing with Peter Golding
Thursday 12th April 2007

We are all born with the ability to dowse, even if we don't realize it is there. It is a natural ability, a sixth sense, but as with most things, you use it or lose it. Children are particularly sensitive when dowsing, and most adults can redevelop the skill at any time.

This was reassuring to members of the Slimbridge Dowsing Group listening to Peter Golding's talk on Thursday afternoon, 12th April. And exciting news for the three new people who had never dowsed before.

After demonstrating deviceless dowsing for which he uses his thumbs – and jolly painful it is too – Peter showed a variety of implements used for dowsing, including metal L-rods and the pendulum which are the most popular, followed by double-V rods made of plastic and the original tool, a hazel twig.

Many people believe dowsing is limited to finding water, but Peter revealed that you can also dowse for oil, lost objects, missing people, the age and whereabouts of archaeological ruins, ley lines, health and healing for both people and animals, remote healing, auras, food allergies, the most appropriate soils in which to plant seeds and even the sex of an unborn baby.

As long as questions only require a Yes or No answer, you can ask virtually anything, such as at the estate agents, "Is this house right for me?" or with various foods, "Is this food suitable for me?" If you receive a "Yes but . . ." answer to that, you might need to ask whether it is alright in this quantity!

You can also dowse to find gas pipes, water pipes and electricity cables in the home, which is a very practical application.

Inviting the new and the inexperienced to the front, Peter took them through the process. "Relax, take a deep breath, think about nothing," he instructed. "Imagine yourself protected by a shield, you don't want to expose yourself to negative energies."

He went on to show how the rods should be held slightly dipped. "Discharge any static by touching your wrists together," he suggested, "and then ask, 'Please may I have my Yes signal?'" The rods almost always turn inwards. Then, 'Please may I have my No signal?' for which the rods usually turn outwards.

"If nothing happens for you," he went on, "it is perfectly legitimate to slightly move your wrist in the appropriate direction, to make it happen deliberately, and familiarise the brain with your Yes and No signals."

Similarly, the pendulum can be 'trained' too. Its chain should be suspended with the fingers pointing downwards, and kept fairly short. Once you have deliberately started it swinging in a straight line, you can ask for your Yes signal and the pendulum will usually swing in a clockwise direction. When asked for the No signal, it will usually swing anti-clockwise.

When this actually worked for the new people, you could see the delight on their faces. Why not try it for yourself? You might be surprised at your own success.

Dowsing and Healing with Joey Korn
Thursday 19th April 2007

When American dowser Joey Korn heard that his neighbour's well had run dry, he simply dowsed the area to find an underground stream nearby. Then, by hammering an iron stake into the ground as directed by his rods, and with intent, he diverted the new stream into the well, where it has been providing a good flow ever since.

That was all in a day's work for Joey, who had some radical ideas to share during his talk on Thursday afternoon, 19th April. While most dowsers are happy to discover water, archaeological ruins or health problems, Joey says, "I see the world as being full of subtle energies. Yes, the space around us is full of radio waves, microwaves, etc., but it is also full of energy lines related to us now and to people who were here before us. And those energy lines spread out in a matrix into the universe."

Joey's talk riveted his audience of 30, who were excited to hear that his dowsing results are substantiated not only by new scientific research and quantum physics, but also by ancient wisdoms such as the power of prayer and positive thinking.

We are aware that nature repeats its own patterns – notably spirals. Joey, whose father Abram was a Holocaust survivor, demonstrated that the people-patterns he is discovering through his dowsing, repeat the configuration of the Cabala, the Jewish Tree of Life. Even though the Cabala has ten emanations or vessels, and the Eastern chakras have only seven, they match when superimposed upon each other.

Since the 1800s, experiments have shown that there is a proven matrix of energies that connects us with everything and everyone. Each of us leaves an imprint of our matrix wherever we go – in our homes, in our beds, even hotel beds and hospital beds.

"Energies can be positive and beneficial," explained Joey, "or they can be negative and detrimental." Consequently, they need re-balancing and Joey believes we can do this with the power of prayer to our own chosen Deity. Our instincts bear this out – for example, saying grace before a meal, saying "Bless . . . !" when someone irritates us, and even saying our prayers before we get into bed.

At the end of the meeting, after a lively question and answer session, many people in the audience were keen to buy a copy of Joey's book, *Dowsing: A Path to Enlightenment*. And while members don't expect to be able to divert underground streams just yet, we can all invoke the power of prayer.

Discoveries at Longbrook Field Iron Age Camp with Peter Gibson – 10th May 2007

When searching for underground ruins and artifacts, archaeologists typically confine themselves to the use of technical surveying equipment and metal detectors. It was therefore a very pleasant surprise for Slimbridge Dowsing Group to receive an invitation from the Dean Archaeological Group to join them in a multi-disciplined survey at the Longbrook Field Iron Age Camp in Churcham, near Minsterworth, last August.

In his talk on Thursday 10th May, Peter Gibson presented a professionally written report on the findings at the site. The farmer, Peter Smart, had kindly agreed that as soon as the crop was cut, they could have access to his field for one month.

Accordingly, archaeologists, surveyors, metal detecting enthusiasts and five dowsers – three from Slimbridge and two from the South Herefordshire Dowsing Group – descended on the huge field in September 2006.

Dowsing quickly indicated a defensive ditch and a wall dating from 300 BC. Roundhouses were also discovered, dating from 1588 BC to 79 BC with 45 dwellings up to 10 metres in diameter, some oval, with associated storage pits. This suggested there were Bronze Age roundhouses as well as Iron Age. There were also three ponds.

Excitement increased as a workshop area with several workshops came to light, apparently used to make pots, metal objects and fences. Three long buildings, possibly for boat construction, were indicated at the southern end of the site, which made sense considering how close the site may have been to the River Severn 2000 years ago.

Two crop growing areas enclosed by a low stone wall were suitable for growing garden crops, and burial areas with graves containing pots with cremated remains in them were to the east of the site. The boundary ditches and walls were intersected by three enormous entrances, plus a smaller one which allowed access to a pond, thought to be of religious significance.

The dowsers felt themselves to be at a significant advantage when dowsing indicated that the original ground level in 300 BC was almost two metres below the present ground level, having been covered by clay and silt over the years. This made it difficult for the metal detectorists who are not able to detect to that depth.

Without wishing to disturb the archaeologists, the dowsers then went on to check the area for less physical evidence, and felt privileged to find a labyrinth dating from 800 BC, several vortexes, some double spirals and two single spirals.

Leylines and earth energies were also in evidence, extremely significant to dowsers, but we had to admit, the archaeologists probably weren't quite ready for them just yet.

Hypnotherapy with Mark Firth
24th May 2007

There was a bit of a hush when hypnotherapist Mark Firth asked for a volunteer who would like to be hypnotised at the meeting on Thursday 24 May, but one intrepid lady, Mavis, was glad of the opportunity.

On an average day, we have as many as 16 million different bits of information coming at us at any one time. The conscious mind can only deal with up to seven things at once, so it is fortunate that the unconscious mind can cope with the rest, filtering, sorting and prioritising before deciding what to allow through for the conscious mind to deal with.

In his talk, Mark of Cygnus Rising Ltd in Dursley, held a large audience in the palm of his hand as he explained how the mind works, how we develop phobias, and how neuro-linguistic programming (NLP) and hypnotherapy can genuinely help us overcome fears and modify behaviours such as smoking and over-eating. "The unconscious mind is a power-house running our entire lives," he said.

Mark stressed that hypnotism can only help us do things we want to do, and feel comfortable about. Despite what we may have seen as entertainment on TV, it cannot make a subject do anything he or she does not want to do.

We all experience events differently, and make judgments depending on our own values and beliefs. Even so, the unconscious process of deleting, distorting and generalising is common to everyone. We all have our own 'map' of the world, built from personal experience, which we use as guidance for how to live our lives.

Mark explained how we can develop a phobia from just one unpleasant experience, for example, with a snake. We might generalise that episode for ever more, believing that to see a snake is frightening and horrible. Yet hypnotherapy, through a light trance, can reach into the unconscious mind and readjust that belief.

It was fascinating to watch Mark, who offers life changing NLP and hypnotherapy through his Dursley and Nailsworth practices, put Mavis into a light trance. Having reassured her that she was perfectly safe, and agreed that her intention was to improve her dowsing skills, he slowly induced the trance, worked with her unconscious mind to generate new options to satisfy the intent, and brought her gently back to the present.

She awoke relaxed and refreshed, and said she had enjoyed the experience very much indeed. Everyone agreed that they had too, and subjected Mark to a lively and lengthy question and answer session.

Green Burial Site Survey – Thursday 14th June 2007

When SDG members recently saw a report in the *Gazette* that a local farmer had submitted to Stroud District Council a planning application to create a green burial site on his land, they thought they might be able to help.

According to the *Gazette* report, Stroud's Planning Department required a site survey to assess whether there was anything of archaeological interest. We immediately contacted the farmer and offered our services.

On Thursday 14th June, a dozen of us descended on the proposed burial site, fanned out across the field and found indications of considerable activity over hundreds of years.

"Throughout Britain there is always a lot to discover," said Peter Gibson, Vice-Chairman and Membership Secretary of the Group. "Most areas have indications of Iron Age and Bronze Age fortifications, agricultural buildings, chantries, churches and ancient burials."

More recent events discovered by dowsing included indications of a crashed airplane 35 years ago, with the loss of two lives, and the fact that the farmer himself suffers from a painful knee! His family was most interested, took a turn with the rods and received some instruction too.

Two of our members are experienced surveyors and will be preparing a report of their findings for the farmer, who will then be in a position to submit details to Stroud District Council.

Animal Healer Ann Lodygowksi
Thursday 2nd August 2007

When renowned animal healer Ann Lodygowski came to talk to us about animal healing, the Gazette *sent reporter Liza-Jane Gillespie to see for herself. They published the following feature on 7th August 2007 with the headline, 'Ann tunes in and talks to the animals'.*

Talking to the animals is usually something reserved for children's imaginations or Dr Dolittle, but a visitor to Slimbridge has shown that it really is possible to chat to your favourite moggy.

According to Ann Lodygowski, communicating with your favourite pet is all about tuning into them. Ms Lodygowski, a dowsing expert, said all she needs is a sample of an animal's hair and she can tune into the animal's emotions and feelings.

"Dowsing is not just about finding water. It can be used for health and also to communicate with animals.

"People can tell you what's wrong but what people don't realize is that animals can as well – you just have to tune in. They have feelings and suffer pain," she said.

The 72-year-old has been communicating with animals since 1976, but she realized she had the ability long before that. "I was 17 when I realised that I could, but I didn't dare tell anyone or I would have been burnt at the stake," she said.

But after years of ignoring her abilities in fear of ridicule, Ms Lodygowski has said now people cannot get enough of her. "I wouldn't be working and people wouldn't ask if they didn't believe it," she said.

Ms Lodygowski works on 18 horses a week, from New Zealand to Canada, diagnosing their problems. On a daily basis she receives letters in the post about all sorts of animals, not just horses.

She said, "I need the hair to tune in to the animal. Then I run my hand over a picture of the skeleton and identify any problems. Sometimes people come to me knowing the problem and I help them find the source."

As well as talking with animals, and helping owners to understand their pet's behaviour, Ms Lodygowski also works with people. "I don't enter anyone's space unless I ask them first," she said.

By entering a person's space Ann Lodygowski can help diagnose a variety of health problems. Colin Davis, 75, of Coaley, is a member of the Slimbridge Dowsing Group and believes Ms Lodygowski helped to diagnose his hip complaint.

He said, "Ann is marvellous. She diagnosed my tilted pelvis and sent me to a chiropractor. I had never seen her before but someone recommended her to me and said she was pretty good. She has also diagnosed my dog as epileptic."

But Ms Lodygowski does still face some hurdles convincing people her information is genuine.

"I was working with a horse in Cornwall and the owner said carp were disappearing from the pond. The horse was in the same field so I asked it questions about the disappearance and got a description of the thief. It was difficult because how do you go to the police and tell them you know who's stealing the carp because a horse told you? They got the person in the end though."

Liza-Jane Gillespie then added a note at the end of the article titled "Meeting Ann Lodygowski". She wrote,

"I walked into Slimbridge village hall as a cynic. I couldn't believe that anyone could talk to animals until I started talking to Ms Lodygowski. To demonstrate her abilities, Ms Lodygowski asked if she could enter into my space and then, using her dowsing stick, she moved her hand across my back and shoulders.

"Within minutes Ms Lodygowski had diagnosed my shoulder problem which I have suffered with for the last few years, but she also noticed a lower back injury which I sustained as a child. To look at me these injuries are not noticeable, and you could say Ms Lodygowski was just lucky, but I left Slimbridge village hall intrigued."

White Witch Toni Hunt
Thursday 16th August 2007

Our speaker on Thursday 16th August was white witch Toni Hunt. She immediately cast a spell over her audience and kept us enthralled for well over an hour. As devout and sincere in her beliefs as any evangelist, she sought not to convince or persuade us, but to open our eyes and our minds to other ideas, thoughts and possibilities.

"In the early days," admitted Toni, "I would have been burnt at the stake." And that is true, since clairvoyance, healing the mind, body and spirit, dowsing, seeing other people's auras, and dealing with paranormal activity, were a definite no-no then, and even today remain unacceptable to many people.

The full car park, however, indicated that there was sufficient interest in Slimbridge to fill the village hall, with more chairs constantly needed.

Early on Toni lead us in a delightful meditation through cool woodland, then asked us what animals we had seen. She was then able to tell us what each animal represented – seeing a dog indicated loyalty, a squirrel meant that person was busy but on someone else's behalf; a big cat peeping out from the bushes suggested that person was non-confrontational.

We were all intrigued by Toni's reports of local paranormal activity. She has visited Woodchester Mansion and the Ram Inn at Wotton-under-Edge with her filming and recording team. Although Toni is the medium, members of her team all heard a woman weeping at Woodchester Mansion, yearning for justice having been murdered many years previously and the murderer never brought to book.

On entering the Ram Inn, Toni realised it had been built on a pagan burial ground and was heaving with overwhelming energies. She calmly said she was stepping outside for a moment, whereupon the owner said, "Most mediums run out of here!"

Toni ended her talk to the loudest round of applause the Slimbridge Dowsing Group has ever mustered, and she is booked to return on Thursday 8th November at 1.30 in Slimbridge Village Hall when she will be talking about paranormal activity. She will show the equipment used and film of investigations. "We have some amazing footage of hauntings," says Toni.

Guesswork and God with George Applegate
Saturday 22nd September 2007

By 10 am on Saturday 22nd September, Slimbridge Village Hall was bulging at the seams. Almost 40 people from far and wide had packed in to hear George Applegate speak.

Author of *The Complete Guide to Dowsing*, and now in his 80s, George began dowsing in 1938. He went to all his dowsing jobs on a Velocette motorcycle and became quite confident. "The biggest danger in dowsing," said George, "is your ego! The best way to learn is from your mistakes, the difficulties and problems. You don't learn from success, which goes to your head."

His first big job was at Mere, where the local water board asked him to find the right spot to sink a borehole that could pump 100,000 gallons per hour. That borehole still supplies Yeovil, Sherborne and the surrounding area today.

Billy Butlin of holiday camp fame, once contacted George urgently, having run out of water with a site full of unhappy campers. Rushing down to Minehead, George found a contractor on site, ready to begin drilling. He duly dowsed and discovered a good underground supply flowing in from the Brecon Beacons. It was so prolific, the Butlin's site now sells a million gallons of water per day to the local authority.

Dowsing for water in Australia was something of a challenge, where they have had no rain for over four years. There was no grass, the livestock were dying, it was a very serious situation. George organised drilling down to 6,000 feet where they found a plentiful supply of water that was 30,000 years old. "It was quite good," he said modestly.

Dowsing for the National Trust on Brownsea Island was relatively straightforward but for one small problem. "A lovely site," said George, "but very expensive to get the drilling rig over there."

Other assignments have included Regent's Park, Wormwood Scrubs prison and Hammersmith Hospital. For George, the most exciting jobs are the ones that go wrong.

"Not because of the dowser," he explained quickly. "Sometimes the driller will drill too fast, which means the spoil does not come up, but goes sideways along the strata, and blocks the flow. Other times, the geology can cause complications."

This modest and charming man delighted his audience with some amusing experiences too. While dowsing in the Cheddar Gorge area, two policemen suddenly appeared and arrested George, convinced he was the poacher they had been seeking for some months. Having no ID on him at the time, George was escorted to the police station from where he was allowed to telephone the Clerk to the District Council, who came and bailed him out.

George's favourite dowsing assignment was in Dorset, not far from Corfe Castle. The site turned out to be a naturist camp, and he had 300 interested but naked people following him around. "Some of them," revealed George, "would have looked better covered up!"

George's pet hate is dealing with "bureaucrats who don't know what they are talking about". Currently he has an assignment in London where finding water has been relatively straightforward, but getting the relevant permissions for various stages has taken nine months so far, and the project still hasn't got anywhere.

George also offers a de-watering service, where he will find out where unwanted water is coming from, and re-route it. He has done this successfully in a skyscraper in New York, a lady's sitting room in Leicester and in the Severn tunnel near Bristol.

Having found water to irrigate a golf course in Japan, hot water for a spa hotel in Bath, and royal water for Prince Charles at Highgrove, George is now turning his attention to oil. As we know, you can dowse for anything if you ask the right questions, and dowsing for oil is quite lucrative.

During a lively question and answer session, everyone was keen to know how George had achieved his unbelievable 99% success rate. "You have to have a strong desire to do it," revealed George. "You have to need to do it. And you have to have faith in yourself that you can do it. It's guesswork and God really."

After signing copies of his book for enthusiastic purchasers, George lead the large group out to the car park, where he demonstrated his method of dowsing for all to see.

Filming the Paranormal with Toni Hunt
Thursday 8th November 2007

As an ex-policewoman, our favourite white witch, Toni Hunt, has been programmed to provide evidence, substantiate her facts and prove anything she claims to be true. When dealing with criminals, that is not always easy, and with paranormal activity, it can be down right difficult.

In a fascinating talk on 8th November at the Royal British Legion Hall in Slimbridge, Toni revealed that, since a riding accident during her time in the mounted police, she had discovered herself to be extremely clairvoyant. She has since enjoyed many courses in healing and communication, so that she is now highly qualified as well as extremely gifted.

In addition to offering healing to people, Toni is also able to communicate with and heal spirits. She explains, "The whole point of communication on the other side is to heal. Spirits can be unrested or unsettled because of injustice or guilt. We as mediators can put some of this to rest."

However, with her police background and training, she seeks to prove the existence of life after life in an evidential way. It is not done for commercial gain but she has made a significant investment in equipment and technology – a mix of clairvoyance and science.

In an entertaining and educational talk, we heard about investigations Toni and her team have carried out at such diverse locations as Woodchester Mansion, the Fleece Hotel in Cirencester, the Speech House Hotel in the Forest of Dean, Berkeley Castle, the Ram Inn at Wotton-under-Edge, Cheddar Caves and Lincoln Cathedral.

Having shown some remarkable infra-red film of hauntings, usually represented by visible orbs, Toni ended the evening with some even more amazing clairvoyance, surprising a couple of members with facts she could not possibly have known in advance.

AGM and dowsing for the NT in Woodchester Park with Barry Goldring – 22nd November 2007

After the boring stuff for the AGM, Barry Goldring gave a fascinating talk about dowsing for the National Trust in Woodchester Park. He had done work for them in the past and they had contacted him again recently, asking him to investigate by dowsing a derelict building known as the kennels.

After some dowsing detective work, it transpired that it had indeed been used as a kennels for fox hounds between 1802 and 1839. Since then, however, it had been used as a stables, possibly as a rest stop during a day's hunting.

Confusingly, the materials used to build the kennels had been recycled from the original Georgian house on the site, and sold to one William Leigh in 1845. It was not until 1857 that he began building the property, which to this day remains uncompleted.

Christmas Party – Come All Ye!
Thursday 13th December 2007

When Arthur Marrow was in Wotton-under-Edge High Street this week, workmen were putting up the town's Christmas lights. Unfortunately, the lights weren't working, so Arthur whipped out his pendulum and diagnosed where the problem was. "It wasn't only a faulty bulb," said Arthur, "it was also an internal break in the cable. I found the spot and once they'd cut and spliced the wires together, it all worked!"

Members heard about Arthur's exploits during Slimbridge Dowsing Group's Christmas party at the Royal British Legion Hall in Slimbridge on Thursday 13th December. It was billed as something different and it was! We were reminded that there are both proper and improper uses for our skills, and dowsing your Christmas presents is definitely not on.

Then our Chairman, Peter Golding, showed a DVD of the film made by National Geographic TV of a day's successful water divining at a farm in Devon last summer. Once Peter's rods had decided on the right place for a borehole, a massive drilling machine was brought in and muddy water was soon spurting everywhere. Filming had taken the whole day, yet the TV slot on 12th November lasted all of three minutes!

After a short talk and some slides from Peter Gibson showing several sites he had dowsed and surveyed during the year, we tried dowsing for a 50 pence piece under three teacups. Interestingly, three of our 'experts' failed at this and several novices met with success. We put an extra 5p under the teacup when the Chairman took his turn so he didn't get it right, but his wife did!

After drinks and nibbles, and exchanging Christmas cards, we wished one and all a Happy Christmas and look forward to an exciting new Programme next year.

2008

Basic Water Divining with Peter Golding
Saturday 26th January 2008

A group of interested dowsers, from absolute beginner to intermediate level, attended a session on basic water divining led by SDG's chairman, Peter Golding.

The morning began with an introductory talk when the basics were explained. The necessity to ask the right questions was stressed. After a chance to practise indoors at the British Legion Club, the group went out onto the playing field.

The course of a stream was located at a depth of 180 feet and, after being pegged out on the ground, was verified by the leader, to the great delight of the participants.

At the end of the morning, the group went back indoors to do some map dowsing.

Drilling for Water in Rhodesia with Gordon Wright
Saturday 23rd February 2008

If any of our members ever thought that a talk on drilling boreholes would be a rather dry subject, then they were in for a pleasant surprise. On 23rd February our guest speaker, Gordon Wright, travelled from Sutton Coldfield to talk about his experiences of drilling for water in Rhodesia. He deliberately didn't refer to it by its present name of Zimbabwe because he said that the country is now completely different from the one in which he was brought up.

Gordon is both a driller and experienced dowser, as was his father from whom he learnt how to find water by holding a forked stick at shoulder height in front of him and observing its reaction when he was near a source of water. It would rotate forward if the source was in front of him, or backwards onto his forehead if behind. He could also estimate the depth by counting the number of rotations it made. However, as his father said, "You can dowse, but you never know if you are right until you drill it."

After many successful boreholes with his father, and feeling very confident, he tried drilling one on his own but failed to strike water after drilling for two weeks through two hundred feet of granite with a slow percussion rig. His father knew perfectly well that he wouldn't find water at that spot but he kept quiet and let him continue drilling a 'dry' borehole, just to teach him not to be over confident.

Gordon explained how he finds the amount of water required for each client's needs. A house may require a hundred gallons per hour, a farmer six hundred, or for crop irrigation, ten thousand. If the latter, then he says you must keep the idea of 'irrigation' in your mind as you search. He said he doesn't like using the same wooden rods twice because they retain a memory of the old well. Sometimes he may need to 'wipe' the memory off them with his hands. Nowadays he uses more durable white nylon dowsing rods.

He went on to describe other methods of finding water. A Nun in Rhodesia would drink a glass of water and then walk over the ground until she felt a sudden urge to 'spend-a-penny'. That was where underground water would be found. If she moved away, then the 'urge' would disappear. It worked!

Pendulum Power with Arthur Marrow
Thursday 13th March 2008

Arthur Marrow has been helping police with their enquiries. He confessed all to the Slimbridge Dowsing Group in Slimbridge Village Hall on Thursday 13th March, during his talk on Pendulum Power.

Although the police are wary of using 'unusual' leads or information, Arthur's reputation is such that he has been able to assist with some quite high profile cases.

Using map dowsing, he is able to establish the whereabouts of stolen property, a body or someone the police are seeking in connection with a crime. By holding his pendulum over letters of the alphabet or numbers one to ten, he can even spell out the name of the street and the number of the house in which the felon can be found.

Arthur feels that dowsing is a precious gift bestowed upon all of us, but like most things, is more highly developed in some individuals than in others.

"As a gift," says Arthur, "I feel we should use it for the public good, and not for personal gain. I like to do it prayerfully for the good of mankind, and to give thanks at the end." Arthur believes if we use the gift to get lottery numbers or forecast the winner of the Cheltenham Gold Cup, we risk losing the ability.

After a lively Question and Answer session, the Group discussed their forthcoming visit to the Ram Inn in Wotton-under-Edge, believed to be Britain's most haunted building. Some members expressed concern about the visit and Chairman Peter Golding reassured everyone that we would meet briefly in the car park beforehand, and dowse so that everyone has a protective shield or cloak. Don't miss the next thrilling instalment!

Ram Inn – most haunted
Saturday 15th March 2008

As regular readers know by now, it is possible to dowse for a variety of things, not just for water, but dowsing for ghosts, corpses, spirals and ley lines is certainly something different. So when the Slimbridge Dowsing Group had the opportunity to visit the renowned Ram Inn in Wotton-Under-Edge on Saturday 15th March to investigate psychic phenomena, seventeen members arrived with divining rods, pendulums and cameras at the ready.

They were welcomed by the owner and custodian for the past forty years, John Humphries, who talked about the history of the place and divulged that TV's Time Team are in negotiations to visit too. There are possible links with William the Conqueror, and the property belonged to the church for a thousand years. Bishops have slept in the Bishop's Room.

After protecting ourselves by dowsing, we explored the grounds and gardens, discovering several hidden archaeological features, and the outline of barns and outbuildings. A pile of masonry was identified as an old mortuary, and a vertical white cross marked the resting place of three sixteenth-century females at a depth of 8 to 9 feet. Buried as pagans, i.e. north-south, they were aged 67, 8 and 69 years.

Nearby was a clear water well, 35 feet deep, vital for any property in those days. The site is at the intersection of two ley lines, also very important to ancient ecclesiastical builders. One ley line goes south towards Ley Farm, Kingswood, and north through St. Mary's Parish Church over Rushmire Hill towards Hetty Pegler's Tump, then through Gloucester and Worcester Cathedrals, both former monasteries.

Dowsing further we found negative and positive energy spirals as well as the old barrel of a cannon dated at 1670. It had been fired in anger, perhaps during the Battle of Nibley Green or the Siege of Wotton Manor House? We also found a passage under the road, linking the Ram to the rear of the church.

Indoors the Victorian parlour was warm and cosy, and through a stone doorway into the oldest part we found the public bar and lounge and a large inglenook fireplace.

The taproom behind the fireplace should have been warm but it felt cold and eerie. By dowsing we soon discovered why – in about 1600 a lady had been murdered there by her brother.

Ascending a creaky wooden staircase we saw many artifacts and the Bishop's Room. Then turning the corner we found an ultra-modern bathroom, complete with corner shower. It was good to know that in such an historic building, with its ghosts and still with wattle and daub from the original wood-framed building, John enjoys a degree of 21st-century comfort. He deserves it.

Dowsing at Coaley Church with Barbara Davis
Thursday 10th April 2008 *(Written by Barbara Davis)*

Intrigued by a recent report in the *Gazette* about a lady who wished her coffin to be taken to Coaley church on an antique bier via a traditional burial route, Slimbridge Dowsing Group felt it would be interesting to dowse the ancient pathway.

Members met at the church on Thursday 10th April, and dowsing revealed that there has been a church on this site since Saxon times, although the current tower is 14th century. As is often the case, the Victorians had added an extension that was not quite as sympathetic as it could have been!

Dowsers found ley lines the length of the church, and were able to establish where the early church had ended, and where the original altar had been. The Victorians had decided the altar should be further back, and replaced the original font with one of their own design but on the same base, 'improvements' that would have provoked a flurry of letters to the *Gazette* Editor in this day and age.

As we entered through the porch, we found a strong spiral that was uplifting, but its 'tail', found further in and to the left of the pillars, was a downward spiral, and not a good place to sit. There were two more spirals either side of the 'new' Victorian altar too.

Running out of time, we ventured outside and dowsed to discover sweet water at a depth of 80 to 110 feet, but bad water at a depth of 20 feet. This is not surprising as water at this level would be subject to pollution, being in the proximity of a graveyard.

It was a remarkable site to dowse and we were delighted to have been sidetracked by so many different energies. Chased home by an April shower, everyone agreed they would have to return to dowse the ancient burial route another day.

Dowsing the Aura with Michael Cook
Saturday 26th April 2008

If you have ever said to anyone, "You're in my space!" it was probably their aura bumping against yours that upset you. Everyone – including animals and plants – has an aura, seven layers of energy surrounding the body in an egg-shape, the same colour spectrum as the rainbow.

At his talk/workshop on 26th April, Michael Cook showed how to test our neighbour's aura. "Open your arms wide," said Michael, "then slowly bring your hands towards their head, where the aura is strongest."

Depending on the size of their aura, which can vary enormously according to mood, health, spirituality, etc., you will soon feel a resistance, as if you were squeezing a balloon. You have to do this gently though, or the person could begin to feel nauseous.

Although scientific research only 'discovered' the aura in the 1700s, many people who were psychic, sensitive or able to dowse (which is most of us if we try!) have been able to 'see' the aura for centuries. Indeed, it is thought that is why Medieval artists painted a halo around the heads of the angels and Jesus, spiritual subjects whose auras were shot with gold. Apparently the aura of the Buddha can be detected 200 miles away.

Each colour represents a different aspect and one or two will frequently dominate. Red is your physical strength and vitality; orange is ambition and responsibility; yellow represents your communication skills and creativity; a bright healthy green shows you are free of money worries but a dark, muddy green means jealousy; blue suggests you are artistic while dominant indigo and violet layers show that you are spiritual and wise. Royalty are supposed to have dominant purple in their auras, which originally indicated a wise leader, but this is not necessarily the case today!

Despite the rainbow rule, other colours can be present too. People suffering from depression will have shades of grey in their auras. The aura of drug-takers can be broken up, with poorly-defined edges and splashes of black throughout. Spiritual leaders will have auras shot with gold and silver. Pink means you are intuitive and aware. A deep magenta red can signify a depraved soul – keep well away!

Experienced practitioners can dowse the state of your aura to see how healthy you are. An isolated black area can suggest cancer, maybe not yet detectable by traditional means. A damaged outer edge will leak energy and you will become more and more tired, even exhausted.

It is possible to offer healing without touching the patient, by simply healing the aura alone. People who have had a limb amputated say they continue to have 'feeling' in the missing limb. The aura around it remains too.

With practise, you can control the size of your aura to some extent. It will shrink if you are closed in or feeling dejected, but expand if you are joyous and outgoing. Each individual layer grows wider. Martial arts experts can even use auric energy to deflect attack!

Our chakras interact with our aura, the energy fields meet, and there is usually a spiral outside that. There are a lot of energy systems around one person and they correspond with acupuncture points.

Certain places can act as an amplifier, and others can decrease or drain your aura. Standing in the pulpit of a church expands your aura and energy ten-fold.

Reiki practitioners treat at the level of the aura, without the need for hands-on healing. Physical problems can be healed in the aura.

There is also a red spot in the centre of the back, directly behind the navel. This signifies you are alive! Our speaker was with someone who had died in an accident, and watched this red spot gradually fade.

The reason we traditionally bring flowers and candles when someone has died, is to disperse the aura, usually allowing three days for the energy to subside. Group members were so fascinated by Michael's talk, the question and answer session at the end lasted for some time, and everyone enjoyed dowsing the colours and band-widths of their neighbour's aura.

Geopathic Stress with Giulia Boden
Thursday 8th May 2008

You can't see it, but this planet is criss-crossed by a global grid of energy fields and forces, ley lines, power spots and spirals. Nothing to do with the electricity company, these are completely natural phenomena which affect us all in subtle ways. Many of them are beneficial, but some are detrimental and can affect our health and well-being.

In her talk on Geopathic Stress on 8th May, Giulia Boden explained that 'geo' means 'of the earth', and 'pathos' translates as 'suffering'. We all know what stress means! Detrimental energies can affect people in different ways – one person will suffer headaches, another person can't sleep and someone else can be totally unaffected – and consequently sceptical and unsympathetic.

Some energy emanating from the earth is so powerful it stresses the immune system. It can affect different areas of your home or workplace (absenteeism), schools (concentration and attention span), and churches (where you feel uplifted). In Hong Kong they build gaps into their skyscrapers in order for such energy to escape.

Dogs will settle happily on beneficial energy lines while cats inexplicably prefer detrimental energy spots. They can feel vibrations that we can't. Even plants respond – herbs and oak trees grow well with geopathic stress whereas roses will not prosper at all.

Members were then given the opportunity to walk around Slimbridge village hall, first to simply feel the ambience, and then with dowsing rods or pendulum. We found a spiral near the stage, and one sensitive lady found evidence of a death in the kitchen – where she regularly makes the tea! It was in the 16th century – long before the hall was built – so we didn't report the matter, but plan to cleanse the area by dowsing without delay.

Reassuringly, there are ways to avoid or ease the influence of geopathic stress. Skilled dowsers can move or shrink energy lines and convert detrimental to beneficial. Crystals can act as a deterrent; earth acupuncture can ease the problem in the form of iron rods hammered into the ground.

There are so many amazing things of which we know so little. Come and join us to find out how much we don't know.

Dowsing for Labyrinths with Peter Gibson
Saturday 24th May 2008

On Saturday 24th May we were fortunate to have the best of the holiday weather for our outside event at Shepherd's Patch, Slimbridge. In a field thought to have been the site of an Iron Age camp, eleven members took on the task of looking for labyrinths, having split into three separate groups.

Labyrinths were usually circular, with turf or stone outlining a path from entrance to centre where believers could meditate, having walked the path following the concentric circles, usually three or seven in number. Seven circuits is the classic and most common configuration, very important in the ancient world since the route in represented the five visible planets, ending in the centre which was Earth. Uplifting energy is felt when meditating there.

The three groups went off in different directions and dowsing identified three labyrinths. One had three circuits, and the other two had seven each. The diameter of the smaller labyrinth was five metres and the other two measured 15 and 17 metres.

Dowsing indicated that the 'walls' had been made of upturned turfs, and dating them suggested one had been built in 92 BC, a second in 370 BC and the most recent, with seven circuits, in AD 1690, having been re-built in the mid-19th century.

Labyrinths were often laid down at fairs in later years but should not be confused with mazes. A labyrinth has only one way in and the same way out, whereas a maze has many passages, some leading to dead ends, and were made for fun and entertainment.

Previous dowsing on the site had indicated an Iron Age camp that had been used for many centuries, with associated sacred areas for healing and worship.

The Bowen Technique with David Tomlinson
Thursday 12th June 2008

Dowsers are interested in a broad range of subjects, and complementary therapies hold a particular fascination. The Bowen Technique, new to most of us at the meeting on Thursday 12th June, was no exception. Bowen practitioner David Tomlinson, based in Wickwar, gave a lively and informative talk, and later demonstrated the technique.

Ideal for sports and work-related injuries, muscular and skeletal pain, and even migraines, the technique was pioneered by Thomas Bowen in Geelong, Australia, in the 1940s and 50s. It first reached England in the 1970s, but it was not until 1992 that one Julian Baker received the treatment in Australia and lost his scepticism – and his pain – overnight. He returned to England and set up the European College of Bowen Therapy, where he sets and assesses the standard for all students.

After outlining the history, David went on to say, "The technique treats the whole person by putting the brain and body back into communication with each other. It allows the body to make changes itself, going back to its normal healthy state."

As further evidence, he pointed out that when you receive treatment for an injury, it can help for a while but, because it has come from outside the body, the pain frequently returns. Whereas the gentle touch of the Bowen technique reminds the brain how to fix the problem from within, and relief lasts significantly longer, often permanently.

The Bowen method is mainly thumbs and fingers performing a rolling-type touch which draws blood to the site for healing, and stimulates lymphatic drainage which transports toxins away. These changes provoke different reactions in different people: some sleep better than they've slept for years, others have unusually clear dreams, everyone develops a strong thirst (water is a necessity after treatment), and most have an urgent desire to empty the bladder.

The two people on whom David demonstrated the technique said they had enjoyed the experience, and felt beautifully relaxed afterwards. "It can be disconcerting for patients when I leave the room during treatment," grins David. "But often it's best to give the treatment and then allow the body time to make the changes it needs without distracting it."

A true case of body, heal thyself – with a little encouragement, of course.

Dowsing Crickley Hill with Liz Poraj-Wilczynska
28th June 2008 *(Written by Barbara Davis)*

Field trips to local sites have proved popular with members this year, and on June 28th a group of us visited Crickley Hill near Cheltenham to be guided around the site by archaeologist and dowser Liz Poraj-Wilczynska (pronounced Bori-Vilchinska!)

She explained the Hill had been occupied since Neolithic times with two separate Iron Age settlements and an earlier village dating from the Dark Ages. The site has been well excavated but the soil layer is very thin, so it is difficult to distinguish between successive occupations. Consequently there is great scope for dowsing to help clarify features and dates.

Guided by Liz we began in the Iron Age settlements. The long house dating from 700 BC and roundhouses dating from 600 BC are marked out on the ground, but we were invited to dowse to see what else we could find.

A series of granaries was indicated and some marked out, plus two watchtowers. We then moved back in time to the Neolithic Period. Liz showed us some flint tools that had been found there.

What may have been the first battle in British history has also been detected at this site – groups of flint arrow heads being an indication that a battle had been fought there. The nearest source of flint is in the Swindon area, suggesting trade in ancient times.

We also dowsed the religious area of the site. Interestingly this was the other side of a ridge and would have been out of sight of the village. Liz showed us the long, artificially-made ceremonial mound. At one time a totem pole stood at one end, and although there is no trace of it now, we were able to dowse its precise location. Our dowsing also located a line of stones along each side of the mound.

Standing at the edge of the promontory, it was easy to see why this had been chosen as a defensive site. The view across the Severn valley towards the Malverns was utterly beautiful.

Dowsing Dursley Castle at the Dursley Festival Sunday 13th July 2008

"Yes, but how do you do it?" was one of the most-asked questions at our stand in the marquee at Dursley Festival on 13th July. The sun shone, the rain stayed away, and we had great fun marking out the site of the long lost Dursley castle on the recreation ground.

Dowsing revealed that the castle was built between AD 1100 and 1200, and was in ruins by the late 1700s to early 1800s. As people entered the recreation ground from the swimming pool car park, and stepped over our markers, we were able to tell them, "You are now in the banqueting hall!" and explain that there were kitchens below. Several people also crossed the moat, but no one got wet.

Typically in the 1800s people would have taken the stone from the castle ruins in order to build elsewhere. We were told a quantity of large stones had been discovered during the recent building work at Rednock School, and wondered whether they could have been from the castle too?

As to how do we do it? Nobody knows! Dowsing is simply an instinctive ability we all had originally, was lost over the centuries, but fortunately handed down within a few families. Rediscover your own dowsing skills – they're in there somewhere.

Wild Plants as Medicine with 'Ben' Stiles
Thursday 10th July 2008

While most of us see wild plants as weeds, dowsers have now learned to see them as valuable yet free medication.

"When we were put on this earth," said Ben Stiles in her fascinating talk on Thursday 10th July, "plants were put here for us for food, and wild plants were put here for us as medicine. We just needed to work out what to do with them, and how to apply them."

Her theme was wild plants as medicine, and Ben's bible is an out-of-print book titled *Health Through God's Pharmacy*. "There's more knowledge in that book than I will ever have!" declared Ben modestly, but she proved to be pretty knowledgeable herself.

She is almost evangelical about the powers of horse-tail (*Equisetum*) which, using sunflower oil as a carrier base, can be applied to an enormous variety of aches and pains. Another favourite is the humble stinging nettle, a diuretic and aid in preventing kidney stones. Picked carefully, and cooked like cabbage, you can eat the leaves and drink the water. Ben also swears by the greater celandine, believing it to be good for varicose and thread veins; dock leaves for burns; mistletoe berries for chilblains; feverfew for headaches and lady's mantle, or *alchemilla mollis*, is great for hair loss.

"These are wonderful plants," enthused Ben, "they do wonderful things." She went on to stress, however, that you need to treat them with respect. Some wild plants are poisonous. "What kills can cure," she says, "and what cures can kill."

This was a reference to homeopathic medicine, where a poison is diluted over and over again to create a healing tincture, usually thirteen times although the best dilution is 21 times. Yet even diluting non-poisonous plants to this extent, in normal quantities can cause the malady they can also cure.

I'm just grateful early man figured out what to do with cocoa beans and made chocolate!

Back to our Roots with Peter Golding
Saturday 23rd August 2008

On Bank Holiday Saturday, we returned to our roots and had a morning water divining in local fields. Led by Chairman Peter Golding, the event attracted several newcomers, who enjoyed a brief introduction in the village hall on the various ways and means of water divining. Peter explained how he always asks his 'higher authority' for permission to dowse, and protects himself with an imaginary shield before he begins.

He also gave a description of each of the rods he uses – L-shaped metal ones, the old traditional hazel twig, and the modern nylon equivalent – and then led us across the road, through the churchyard and into the field beyond.

Everyone then enjoyed doing their own water

divining; most of us found a water course some 60ft down, flowing diagonally across the field. It is an enormous thrill when you try dowsing and your rods move for the first time. You can't quite believe it, yet you have seen it with your own eyes – and felt it too.

It was delightful when a dozen or so milking cows suddenly joined us in the field, the sun shone, and Peter then showed us how to establish the depth of the water, firstly by measuring the distance between two parallel dowsing reactions, which he called the 'Bishop's Rule', or simply by asking 30ft? 40ft? 50ft? 60ft? When the rods swing inwards for Yes, you have the answer.

The main purpose of water divining is to determine where to drill a borehole for a source of underground water for farmers, private residences or private companies. And there are quite a lot of geological considerations too, such as whether there is clay under foot, which may hold water but does not release it, whether there is gravel, or even if there is an underground cave. If you drill too deep, could you lose it all into a chasm below?

It's a big responsibility to tell a farmer, "Yes, this is the place to spend several thousand pounds on drilling and sinking your borehole." What if you are wrong?

Untangling the String Theory with Marcus Burnett
Thursday 11th September 2008

For a talk that was booked several months ago, our speaker on Thursday 11th September was surprisingly topical. Bristol-based Marcus Burnett, a talented Medium for over 20 years, spoke about current scientific research into psychic phenomena. He mentioned the controversial so-called Big Bang experiment at CERN in Switzerland that had been switched on just the day before, and believes their results will support current research into the String Theory.

For many years, science, religion, dowsers and psychics had little common ground, and no real common language with which to communicate. However, the String Theory is relevant to each and every one of us.

Put simply, the String Theory postulates that everything is a living, vibrating force. Scientists accept that this force or energy or vibration – call it what you will – is throughout all things. The universe is made of just one thing – energy – but vibrates in very different ways. We can all know and perceive a vibrating force, even if it is too small to detect physically. This substantiates the ancient idea that all life is connected.

Quantum physics already proves in many ways that this is a reality. Scientists were sceptical for some time, but the String Theory proves all their theories, for example, gravity. And now that there is an elegant mathematical formula, they are more comfortable with the concept. Another sticking point for them is that the String Theory also embraces the idea of a Divine Architect. Yet it makes sense that these vibrations come from a main creative force.

Even more interestingly, the String Theory postulates that there is a Super String, a force so intense that it could well prove to be the soul, or our consciousness. The vibrations of this Super String are so fast and powerful, it could simply be our true self, and scientists have detected some physical evidence in the pineal gland. It is thought this Super String is what enables us to connect with all other levels and aspects of life, as long believed by religion and psychics.

Although this is difficult to understand – and even more difficult to write about! – it has created common ground and a common language between all factions. We live in exciting times and it is comforting to know that the scientists are finally coming round to our way of thinking!

AGM and The Battle of Evesham with Peter Gibson 13th November 2008

AGMs are renowned for being boring, but ours was brief, and no-one actually went to sleep. Committee members gave the usual reports and we learned that our paid-up membership has now increased to 39 plus many visitors, mainly thanks to the *Gazette*, which is very good to us and includes our activity reports and photographs on a regular basis. The same old faithfuls were re-elected yet again, and the new Committee looked suspiciously like the old one.

The AGM was followed by a talk from member Peter Gibson about some archaeological dowsing research he had recently done for the Simon de

Montfort Society in Evesham. They were keen to find indications of a chapel and a spring thought to have healing properties, on the famous site of the Battle of Evesham, which took place in 1265.

There being no physical evidence remaining, dowsing was their best hope. Accompanied by Barry Goldring, Peter Golding and Rex Brice, Peter had visited the site and met with gratifying success.

The whole area had at one time belonged to the Abbey, and there is still an Abbey Farm nearby. They quickly located a well with a font not far away, and then a sacred area with an altar or shrine beside the main path.

Continuing their investigations, they found indications of a chapel but the dates were not right. This was something of a red herring, probably a pagan religious building because the altar was on the north side. They later found indications of another chapel and on asking for the dates, dowsing reaction suggested this was the right one, particularly as there was a leyline running through it, suggestive of a religious building. There were four leylines crossing the site, connecting it with the Abbey itself, some distance away.

On a second visit, bearing in mind that a battle would have produced a significant number of bodies, Peter searched for and found indications of a large mass grave. This was substantiated by the fact that there was no grass in that area, simply broadleaf weeds. The energy there was not good, with several negative spirals. Evesham folk confessed they did not like to go there, especially the man responsible for cutting the grass.

Further dowsing around the chapel discovered a grave before the altar. Peter wondered if it might be that of Simon de Montfort himself, but Barry's dowsing rods told him it was the remains of a child. Physical artefacts from the 13th Century were now at some 3 metres below the current ground level, so a dig would be a major undertaking.

The Simon de Montfort Society had also invested in a geophysical company to do depth soundings and resistivity tests. When Peter showed their plotted results compared to his own, there were many consistencies and matching areas.

"We look for walls and they look for rubble," said Peter. Both had obtained similar results although dowsing was more detailed – and cost nothing but a flask of coffee and a pleasant day out.

Hypnotherapy with Mark Firth
Saturday 22nd November 2008

Hypnotherapy was the subject of a talk at our meeting on Saturday morning 22nd November. Our members relaxed in the comfortable venue of the Slimbridge Royal British Legion club whilst ex-Navy helicopter instructor Mark Firth, speaking in a deep, soothing voice, and well chosen words, described how hypnosis can be used to help overcome mental and physical disorders.

Mark said there was a great similarity with dowsing, and started by asking us to hold our rods or pendulums and consider how we feel when waiting for a dowsing reaction. He said this feeling of detachment and concentration is effectively the same in hypnosis. All hypnosis is self-hypnosis – becoming focused and detached whilst remaining alert. This acts as a tool to access the subconscious mind to accept subtle instructions.

Whereas our conscious mind controls many of our activities such as movement, speech, eating, etc., the unconscious mind runs such vital activities as heartbeat and general maintenance and repair of the body. In the unconscious mind, there is a model of how the body should work – like a designer's blueprint. The unconscious mind will control our involuntary systems to make the necessary adjustments to ensure we function in accordance with that model.

Sometimes, when we suffer pain for example, hypnosis can access the subconscious which, by responding to suggestions by the hypnotherapist, can adjust the bodily systems to alleviate pain.

Can hypnotherapy help one to lose weight? Mark's suggestion is, "Stop eating when you've had enough!"

Four Tables Dowsing – Christmas Party 2008
11th December 2008

What do dowsers do at Christmas? Have fun, of course! For our Christmas party on 11th December, we had a Four Tables event, but in our case it was five.

Members and guests were able to visit each table in turn and using either their L-rods or pendulum, had a go at map dowsing to find an extinct village between Tetbury and Cirencester (inhabitants had died out during the plague in the 1600s); finding the electrical faults in a run of Christmas tree lights; dating pottery (one piece believed to be from the 13th century); remote viewing and checking on food allergies and intolerances.

The remote viewing was the most challenging. We were given a selection of envelopes, each containing a picture of a famous landmark somewhere in the world, and by simply holding it, had to report the images that came into our minds. This was the first time for most of us, so we didn't do too well, but as with most things, the more you do it, the better it gets.

The allergies and intolerances table, run by our Chairman, Peter Golding, was one of the most popular. By simply touching a selection of foods one at a time – bread, coffee, eggs, dairy produce, an orange, a tomato, etc. – our L-rods or pendulums would indicate whether we had a true allergy or merely an intolerance. Peter then went on to ameliorate the reaction in the hope of balancing the sufferer and make it safe to try the suspect foods. One delighted lady ceased to react to fish and another now seems safe to try oranges again after many years without.

Our fifth table was filled with exciting-looking Christmas presents, provided by one generous member, Jim Greatrix. We had to dowse asking,

"Which is the most suitable Christmas present from Jim to me?" Several rods responded to bottles of wine and chocolates, but no one picked up on the packet of cigarettes, which tells you a lot about dowsers!

Once we'd tried our hands at the tables, we moved on to checking out each other's chakras and auras. This was great fun – one member was found to have an enormous aura measuring over 12 feet, and another member was delighted to learn all her chakras were in balance, which is actually quite unusual.

It was at this meeting that the first edition of our brand new Newsletter was distributed. It showed the programme for most of the forthcoming year, 2009.

2009

Stepping into the Breach with Goldring & Golding
Thursday 8th January 2009

Disaster! When the guest speaker you booked almost a year ago, falls ill and has to let you down at the last minute, it's a daunting task to suddenly produce a suitable replacement at very short notice. Several frantic phone calls and panic-stricken e-mails later, we had cobbled together a fine programme that was enjoyed by all.

Treasurer Barry Goldring stepped into the breach and updated us regarding the dowsing investigations he has been doing for the National Trust at Woodchester Park. Barry has been watching too many *Time Team* programmes, and made his talk into a detective story.

He described a very fine but overgrown wall he and the warden had inadvertently discovered near the park's boundary. It was all a great mystery, and Barry built up the excitement by describing their initial thoughts, suspicions and the questions he asked of his dowsing rods.

Regular readers will know you can ask your dowsing rods anything you like as long as the answer is Yes or No. So it took some time, quite a lot of digging and the discovery of some intricate drainage channels, to establish that what they had found was – wait for it – a 1779 sheep dip.

Just as we could all breathe a sigh of relief as the mystery was solved, Barry revealed that, beneath some of the undergrowth, he and the warden had then discovered another drain of Roman origin. Don't miss the next thrilling instalment.

After this we were ready for a bit of relaxation, so Chairman Peter Golding showed a video of a 1982 ITV programme with the late Roy Talbot. Interviewed by one Alan Jones, who kept his arms folded throughout, Roy revealed a great deal about water divining and his methods for sinking boreholes, usually for farmers.

While ITV presenters may well have improved their body language over the years, it was comforting to find that dowsing has changed very little. At least one person left the meeting saying, "I enjoyed that. Let's hope another speaker cancels soon!"

The Pendulum Paradigm with Ian Critchley
Saturday 24th January 2009

We never cease to be amazed at what our bodies and minds are capable of, how they protect us and know what is best for us, far better than we can know ourselves.

In his talk on neuro-linguistic programming (NLP) on 24th January, Ian Critchley explained that he does not use the dowser's pendulum to hypnotise people, but for getting in touch with the inner recesses of the mind. After 12 years with Magnox at Berkeley, Ian has retrained as a life coach, working with people to raise their awareness and to work out what they want to achieve. This is done through the unconscious mind, and the pendulum is a useful tool for communicating.

The unconscious mind is minutely aware of our state of health and can heal from within, in order to preserve our bodies and minds as best it can. It genuinely wants the best for us and even uses telepathy when needed. This is more developed in some individuals than others, and comes in very useful when dowsing.

"No hypnotist, how ever skilled he might be, can make anyone do anything outside their core values and beliefs," says Ian reassuringly. "These come from conditioning in childhood, and make us who we are and behave the way we do."

Equally, we can also have unresolved problems embedded in the unconscious mind, which is how phobias begin, even if we cannot consciously remember them. Indeed, the human memory can be quite selective, and simply refuse to remember experiences that are too painful or uncomfortable to deal with at a conscious level.

Ian explained that it is important to maintain a balance when helping people with phobias. He cannot entirely remove, for example, a fear of heights or fire, or a patient might end up taking unnecessary risks. Fear and anger have a purpose and suppressing them – frequently necessary in today's society – can be extremely stressful.

Everything we experience is recorded in our subconscious and stays with us until we die. It becomes more difficult to access as it as it goes deeper into our subconscious, but it is always there.

Demonstrating on a couple of volunteers brought some interesting results, particularly when Ian raised the metabolic rate of one lady. This was your classic 'Do not try this at home' experiment, but a member of the audience was invited to take the lady's pulse, and was amazed to find it almost doubled from an unusually low 60 to a relatively rapid 120.

During a lively question and answer session at the end, someone asked about Time Lines. These are your perception of the past and of the future, most commonly envisaged with the past behind us and the future ahead, although not everyone sees them that way.

During a life coaching session, Ian will ask the 'patient' to envisage his time line, how it looks, what colour it is, and the location of things that have happened along its length. Once identified, it is possible to make adjustments, which can help people let go of something bad in their past and, having dealt with it, move on.

Aura Soma Essential Oils with Melanie Lewis
Thursday 12th February 2009

Regular readers will already know that dowsers believe the subconscious mind knows what is best for the body. This includes food, medicines, healing, colours, all sorts of things. The idea was demonstrated very powerfully when Melanie Lewis visited us on Thursday 12th February to talk about Aura-Soma oils and unguents. Members were invited to choose from 106 beautiful bottles containing two liquids: the top half was a highly perfumed olive oil derivative containing essential oils, and the lower half is the purest water that can be found, purified again, and both in the loveliest jewel-like colours.

As we all learned at school, oil and water don't mix, so the two remain separate unless vigorously shaken to form an emulsion and even then, separate out again very quickly. However, there is more to these liquids than meets the eye because they are imbued with healing properties from crystals. The colours match those of our seven chakras, which echo the colours of the rainbow, and you are very much the colours you choose.

For example, someone who has recently suffered a bereavement, is not sleeping well, and feels stressed, is very likely to choose the deep blue oil with a pretty pink water. This is the subconscious mind choosing what it needs – lavender, which is associated with relieving all those things, and pink which brings with it kindness, caring, warmth and being gentle with yourself.

For dowsers, however, the exciting part was when Melanie invited a couple of volunteers to select the colours that spoke to them, (colour blind and blind people can intuitively choose too), and briefly hold them. Our most experienced dowser, Chairman Peter Golding, asked his rods to show the edge of the aura of each volunteer before they chose their colours, and again after they had briefly held them to the heart. The increase in the size of the aura before and after – denoting an increase in wellbeing – was measurably significant, at least 9 or 10 inches.

There are different products for different purposes, such as a paint additive, shower gel, pomanders and quintessences. They are quite expensive to buy and you need a consultation with an experienced practitioner, but this was not a selling exercise. Melanie was happy to simply tell us, a receptive audience, about these wonderful products. And even the most determined cynic could not deny, they smelled absolutely wonderful.

Kinesiology with Janet Nicholls
Saturdayn 28th February 2009

They say seeing is believing, but in the case of kinesiology, feeling is believing too.

At our Saturday morning meeting on 28th February, Janet Nicholls from Abergavenny gave a fascinating talk and workshop about kinesiology, otherwise known as Touch for Health, the study of movement. However, that study – a combination of chiropractic methods and Chinese medicine – is predominantly of the muscles, and can reveal a great deal about a patient and their symptoms.

Testing is through muscle resistance, and Janet soon had us all on our feet, testing each other. In pairs and in turn, we were instructed to match pressure from our partner's forearm. "Think of something that makes you happy," she ordered, and muscle response was steady and strong. "Now think of something that makes you sad," she said, and immediately our muscles weakened and became a bit 'wibbly-wobbly'.

As dowsers, we wanted to know how it worked. Muscle response is apparently related to the meridians throughout the body, and to the lymphatic system. The human body is very susceptible to blockages in one way or another, and kinesiology is a valuable resource for identifying the problem and, over time, resolving it too. "It's not about a quick fix," says Janet.

And yet, one lady who had hobbled in with severe discomfort from six-month-old whiplash, exacerbated by yesterday's bike ride, was surprised to find her ear being massaged, and prompt relief. After half an hour, she was able to turn her head significantly further than previously, with much less pain.

Another member who has been troubled by painful arthritis for many years, was invited to hold a carton of milk to her cheek, in close proximity to the saliva gland, while her muscle resistance was checked.

"You have an intolerance to cow's milk," confirmed Janet, "and to goat's milk, and to sheep's! Ah, you're OK with soya milk. If you switch to soya milk, you will find your arthritis considerably relieved."

Our speaker had learned this the hard way herself many years previously. She had been 3 stones overweight and thoroughly depressed. Muscle testing revealed that she was intolerant of milk and wheat.

"But I can't be!" she protested, "I'm a farmer's wife!"

But she was, and within three months she had shed her extra weight, and was feeling happy and energised.

All sorts of things can unbalance the physical body, the mind, the equilibrium. Just think how often you are exposed to things your body can't tolerate: foods, car fumes (bad), flowers (good) . . . and the effect they can have. Fears and phobias too are the result of an imbalance, and can be helped by kinesiology.

The joy of Touch for Health is that we can also help ourselves. The whiplash lady can massage her own ear; the arthritis sufferer can control whether she drinks cow's milk or soya; we can knowingly avoid breathing in fumes; we can take balancing exercise and we can certainly increase our consumption of water.

Bach Flower Remedies with Daphne Adams
Thursday 12th March 2009

Our 12th March meeting began in a most unusual way when Daphne Adams, our speaker, passed round a bottle of Bach's Rescue Remedy for everyone to take four drops on the tongue and get themselves in a receptive mood. She described how Dr Bach, a medical practitioner in Birmingham, became disillusioned with conventional medicine and in the 1930s turned his back on his profession and went to live in a cottage with a garden in Oxfordshire.

Dr Bach, a very religious man, felt drawn to natural remedies and began to experiment using the plants found growing locally. He developed 38 remedies for use in different situations and felt that a cure was effected by treating a person in two ways – the type of person they are and the situation they are currently in.

Thus a treatment consists of a small bottle filled with spring water and a little brandy as a preservative, plus a teaspoonful of the relevant mix of remedies. One bottle can last for three weeks as the remedy is taken as four drops four times a day. The remedies cannot be overdosed but can be under-dosed and therefore not effective.

Daphne Adams, herself an accomplished dowser, astonished the meeting by saying that the remedies should not be dowsed for. Dowsing goes to the heart of the matter but the Bach Remedies treat each stage one at a time, so the Remedy needs to be changed as the situation alters.

Remedies have no side effects and can be used on animals and in conjunction with medicines prescribed by doctors. Even plants will respond to having a dose of Rescue Remedy! At the conclusion of the meeting members were able to browse through some of the books written by Dr Bach.

Water Divining with Peter Golding
Saturday 28th March 2009

What should you do when you arrive for a meeting and find everyone waiting outside because the door is locked? This was the situation when members arrived at the Slimbridge RBL Club on Saturday 28th March for Chairman Peter Golding's talk on Water Divining.

We didn't know where to find the caretaker to let us in, and another group was using the Village Hall, so we decided to go to church! We had held meetings in Slimbridge church before, so we knew it was a suitable venue. We deposited our dues in the church wall box instead of into Dowsing Group funds.

Water divining can be a dry subject, but Peter made it interesting and began by outlining simple basic procedures. He said it is pointless searching for water if the subterranean rock is not capable of storing water, and listed rocks that make good aquifers and those that don't. Fortunately, most areas of Slimbridge are on a thin layer of water-bearing gravel between layers of clay, so we had a good chance of detecting where water could be found if drilling a borehole a few metres deep.

We then went into a nearby field and dowsed for an underground stream. We searched for a second one that crossed it but at a different level, thereby doubling the chance of not merely finding water, but providing an adequate flow rate too. Most of us were able to do this and Peter confirmed our results, as he is a professional water diviner.

He then demonstrated how to predict the depths of the underground streams and how many gallons per minute could be expected. There are two useful methods for predicting the depth, the Bishop's Rule and Creyke's Rule, whereby you walk away at right angles to the source until your dowsing rods react. That distance is equal to the depth at which water will be found.

At the end of the exercise, Peter asked us to get in a line alongside him and walk together towards the underground stream where each one of us found our dowsing rods reacted at the same point. He suggested we call this 'line dowsing'!

To finish off the morning, Peter showed us where there was a powerful and beneficial spiral of earth energy rising from the ground. It caused our rods to rotate like a windmill, and we experienced an uplifting warm feeling: an excellent place for lovers to embrace.

Earth Energies with Peter Gibson
Thursday 9th April 2009

There are spirals everywhere. It's one of nature's most repeated and strongest patterns. You can see spirals in sea shells, on a snail's back, in plants and their seeds, notably the pine cone, as well as in cacti, corals and even the solar system. Man copied the idea – notice the strength of a spiral staircase.

Why is it so surprising then, that spirals also emanate from the ground as an earth energy? They spiral upwards as positive energy, tower above us, then topple over and spiral downwards as negative energy.

Although they aren't visible to the naked eye, we dowsers find them all over the place with our dowsing rods, and happily watch our rods turning full circle, rapidly in a strong one, more slowly in a weaker one.

We stand in the uplifting part, avoid the down draft, and notice with wonder how the positive spiral usually comes from a patch of longer grass and the negative downward part returns to a patch marked at this time of year by daisies.

Our speaker Peter Gibson then went on to talk about earth energies in general, but spirals were the star of the show. Dowsing rods are one of the few methods able to detect such phenomena, which has been known and recognised since before Nostradamus was a boy (1503–1566).

Reflexology with Isobel Willmott
Saturday 25th April 2009

There is an ancient cave drawing in Egypt that depicts two men practising reflexology on two patients, and it dates from 2330 BC.

The ancient art remained in use in China, Japan, India and throughout the Eastern world but, as usual, was lost to Western medicine until the 1960s. Once we rediscovered it, we embraced it, and inevitably set up an Association of Reflexologists, but what is it and how does it work?

In her talk on Saturday, 25th April, trained reflexologist (and dowser) Isobel Willmott from South Herefordshire Dowsers, revealed that there are principal reflexes on the feet and hands that correspond to every part of the body. So it is possible to work on any part of the body by manipulating the feet or, less usually, the hands.

Reflexology can be extremely beneficial, confirmed Isobel, as it encourages the body to heal itself. It balances the system, releases toxic waste, and helps blood to flow more freely, which in turn brings more oxygen to the tissues and makes us feel better.

It can be a useful diagnostic tool too, although it is continually drummed in to dowsers, reflexologists and alternative practitioners alike that only qualified medical practitioners can make a diagnosis. But puffiness, local tenderness, and discolouration – including redness and even yellow – are strong clues to a patient's physical and emotional wellbeing, and an experienced reflexologist will easily identify them.

What is it good for? It is wonderful for helping you relax, so very good for stress, and 75% of dis-ease is stress related.

Those suffering from MS and ME find it helpful, as do sufferers of sinus problems, digestive disorders, hiatus hernia and even fertility problems.

Sometimes a malady will become worse before it gets better and other reactions can include a patient becoming emotional during treatment, a lowering of body heat, feeling sleepy and, as it aids the flow of fluids, an urgent need to pop off to the loo.

There are, of course, things it is not so good for, and practitioners are wary of treating diabetics, early pregnancies, those with metal rods or plates inserted surgically, and various cancers, although again it can be supportive and therapeutic for cancer sufferers in the terminal stages.

Isobel demonstrated the process on two or three volunteers, one of whom felt immediate relief in his back.

Relieving Geopathic Stress with Peter Golding
Thursday 14th May 2009

Regular readers will know that everything on this earth is comprised of energy, and it all vibrates at different frequencies. Sometimes this is good and sometimes it's not so good.

The earth emits a natural electromagnetic field that is beneficial – indeed, necessary – for all biological beings, i.e. those dependent on oxygen. Unfortunately, this beneficial energy can sometimes become corrupted by such natural phenomena as underground flowing water, fault lines, changes in rock strata or mineral beds.

This can result in detrimental, even hazardous, energy vibrations, affect people and animals adversely, and is known as Geopathic Stress (GS). You may have noticed for yourself that some places feel good, uplifting, whereas other places can feel oppressive and unpleasant.

In his talk on Thursday, 14th May, Chairman Peter Golding explained that if your bed or your favourite arm chair happens to be over such stress lines, you can feel unwell, depressed, suffer from lack of sleep or become seriously ill.

Cancer is often associated with this phenomenon, as are arthritis, MS, sudden infant death syndrome (SIDS), insomnia and chronic fatigue.

Yet interestingly, these adverse vibrations are good for bacteria and fungus, which will actually thrive. Cats are drawn to it too, whereas dogs will avoid it at all costs.

A couple sharing a home affected by GS might find one of them is affected and not the other. Frequently, women seem more sensitive to GS, thought to be because their ovaries will resonate at a different frequency from that of the male prostate.

If this sounds like so much mumbo-jumbo to you, you should have been there! Peter first dowsed for a GS line in the Slimbridge Village Hall. He then dowsed the auras of a couple of volunteers standing outside the GS line, and again within it. Even the largest auras were diminished to some degree.

An experienced dowser such as Peter can move or 'heal' such lines, and convert the negative energy to beneficial. If the cat comes to sit on your lap every evening, it might be worth getting your home checked for GS. There are plenty of expensive meters and 'magic boxes' on the market, but all you really need is a pair of dowsing rods.

Dowsing Thistledown with Barry Goldring
Saturday 23rd May 2009 *(Written by Barbara Davis)*

Bank holiday Saturday, May 23rd, found Slimbridge Dowsing Group at Thistledown Environmental Centre, near the Nympsfield windmill, on our first field trip of the year. It was a bright if somewhat breezy morning, so we decided to erect a tent for shelter. This proved to be the biggest challenge of the day! Dowsing rods are useful for many things but erecting tents is not included. With a battle against the wind and the instructions, it took six members an hour to erect it.

After a well-deserved coffee break, the rest of the morning was spent doing our own investigations into the energies of the Thistledown stone circle, or walking in the surrounding woodland. The stone circle is not an ancient one, but just the fact that it is there has created interesting energy levels within and around it.

After lunch we were joined by family groups camping at the site, who were probably far better at erecting tents than we were. After an initial chat about dowsing, we supplied them with dowsing rods and encouraged them to try it for themselves. Within a short time, cries of, "It actually works!" and "I can do it!" could be heard. We showed them how healing energy can be applied and then they tried dowsing for underground flowing water.

Much encouraged, they moved on to the stone circle to investigate the energies there. As is often the case, the younger family members proved very proficient at dowsing, and declared they would practise when they got home.

Berkeley Castle dig with Arthur Marrow
Monday 8th June 2009

There's too much stuff to learn in this world. We had a glimpse of just how much on 8th June when we were invited to dowse an archaeological dig in the grounds of Berkeley Castle. It was a history lesson, an archaeology lesson and a dowsing lesson all in one.

It was a privilege to be allowed in, since traditionally archaeologists don't have a lot of time for dowsers. With all their sophisticated equipment, experience and qualifications, they view our dowsing rods and skills rather like the medical profession used to regard chiropractors and acupuncture. As both are now available on the NHS, dowsers live in hope that one day archaeologists will accept dowsing too. It would save the students a lot of digging!

To be fair, Professors Dr Mark Horton and Dr Stuart Prior, seen on Channel 4's *Time Team* but also lecturers at the University of Bristol and directors of the three on-going Berkeley Castle digs, were open minded about dowsing, and happy for us to go ahead.

"And if you can locate the market cross shown on Henry VIII's Tudor map dated 1541, that would be most helpful," said Stuart.

The confusing thing for archaeologists is the layers upon layers of history beneath our feet. Stuart took time to point out various levels in the soil across the site, from 21st and 20th century at the top, then 19th to 18th Century garden earth, then the 17th century layer during which Berkeley Castle was the site of much civil war activity (1641–1651).

Lower still, we could see the level floor of a hall with stones marking a semi-circular hearth, thought to be Saxon (AD 597–1066). There was a stone road beside it with a few Roman red bricks sticking up like old teeth, which were probably already there, and used as rubble or hardcore by the Saxons.

Yet for dowsers, what you ask for is what you get, and if we ask for, say, a religious building of the Saxon period, our rods respond to that alone. There might be layers of history in between, but our rods won't react to anything else until specifically requested to do so.

We were able to dowse and find where the Saxon road ended, (not much further to go, chaps), and Barry Goldring dowsed and recorded three Saxon houses, even though Stuart was only expecting two.

Peter Golding established an area where there had been several burials in the 700s. Opinion was divided as to whether this was a church or simply a burial ground.

Later we headed off to the area believed to be the site of the market cross but had mixed success. Some of us found two, one built in the 700s and long gone by the 12th century, and a second, further over, that was there in 1541 and likely to be the one on Henry VIII's map.

Yet another member, David Excell from Hereford Dowsers, dowsed and found a market cross almost under the boundary wall. So the jury is still out on market crosses.

We hope to return and do more work on this. The great thing about dowsing an archaeological dig is that one day it will be completed and we will know whether we were right or wrong.

Location, Location, Location with Arthur Marrow
Thursday 11th June 2009

Lost, stolen or strayed? Whether you are looking for your missing spectacles or a dead body, dowsing can find them. There was a record turnout of over 30 people for Arthur Marrow's talk on Thursday, 11th June, so perhaps they'd all lost something too?

As we like to joke, Arthur is renowned for helping the police with their enquiries, and although this sounds quite glamorous, Arthur takes a very prosaic and organised approach.

"Always use a checklist," he says firmly, "and write out the numbers 1 to 10 on a piece of paper, plus 100, 200, etc. On another piece of paper, write down all the letters of the alphabet, and on a third, draw a cross and mark the points of the compass, north, south, east and west." Now we've set out our stall, we can begin.

Firstly, focus the mind very strongly on the object or person you are seeking. Thinking hard, write down and dowse over such simple questions as What, Where and When. Photographs can be useful too. Using your pendulum or rods, and your prepared sheets of paper, phrase your questions so that they can be answered 'Yes' or 'No'. Double check everything and finally, instructs Arthur, make good notes afterwards.

When asked to help find a missing young girl in the north of the country some months ago, Arthur started with the compass points, and his pendulum found she was in the southwest quadrant, just a couple of miles from home. Her subsequent discovery, safe and well, proved him correct.

When Barry George was convicted of Jill Dando's 1999 murder, Arthur dowsed and felt there had been a miscarriage of justice. Dealing directly with the Home Office, subsequent events proved him right. He has also made private predictions regarding the missing farmer's wife from west Gloucester, and on the disappearance of little Madeleine McCann, but both cases remain sub-judici so we must await the outcome.

On other occasions, Arthur helped police locate a massive stash of stolen items, just as they were about to be shipped abroad. And by dowsing the alphabet written on one of his precious sheets of paper, Arthur was able to spell out the address many miles away in London of a felon the police were seeking. They rushed round to the address and there he was!

Yet Arthur is a modest man and reports his failures as well as his successes. A friend recently asked him to locate her wedding ring, missing for several years. He dowsed and found traces of where it had been, but could not find where it is today.

Honest to a fault, our speaker also confessed that he had once tried to dowse lottery numbers, but was told if he used his skills for personal gain, he might lose them. So he does not do that any more.

During a lively question and answer session, someone asked whether dowsing is learned, or whether you are born with it. The answer is, we are all born with the ability to dowse, and we can all do it – until we're told we can't.

A Visit to Avebury with Peter Golding and Isobel Willmott – 27th June 2009

How did he know? Stone Age man must have realised there was a good reason to build what is still the largest stone circle in the world at Avebury in Wiltshire 5,000 years ago, but how?

He was quite right, of course. There is a pair of leylines or currents of male and female energy that run from St Michael's Mount in Cornwall to East Anglia, so strong they have been named the Michael and Mary lines. They link many sacred sites en route but, significantly, they actually cross at Avebury.

This crossing makes for a highly powerful surge of energy, and our dowsing rods were responding very strongly before we'd even asked a question! Stone Age man definitely knew what he was doing. It was no coincidence he chose this site – long before Stonehenge was even on the drawing board.

A group of twenty of us from Slimbridge Dowsing Group and South Herefordshire Dowsers met up for our first field trip of the summer on 27th June to investigate this remarkable place.

Blessed with superb weather, we donned sunhats and suncream, and set off to explore, rods whizzing and brains reeling.

The Avebury site, built about 2600 BC, is a large 'henge', being enclosed by an earthwork bank and a massive internal ditch, with an outer stone circle and two inner ones.

Or, more accurately, the remains of, because over the centuries, the local population managed to destroy many of the stones, either to use them for building houses or simply to get them out of the way of their plough. One man got his come uppance when a stone he was trying to topple, fell and crushed him to death. Nearby coins dated 1320 conveniently date that incident.

As with Stonehenge, we're not perfectly certain why Avebury was built, or what it was used for. The southern inner circle was dedicated to the sun and the northern inner circle to the moon.

Human bones have been found, which indicates burial and worship on a large scale. Human sacrifice is a possibility as it has been a spiritual centre for Pagans, Wicca, Druids and Heathens. There is undoubtedly some connection with nearby Silbury Hill, Glastonbury, the later Stonehenge and, for all we know, the ongoing and extensive crop circle activity in the area too.

While the sun was at its zenith, we retreated to the cool of the church to dowse the energies there. Churches are frequently built on what was originally a pagan site, with first a humble wooden building, and later something more permanent and magnificent.

Consequently there are always strong energy lines to be found, and Avebury church did not disappoint. One leyline in particular, that passed through the font, was strong enough to send our dowsing rods into overdrive.

We cannot claim on this occasion to have come up with any answers, but we certainly enjoyed our day and came up with a whole host of new questions.

We realise now, Stone Age man knew a lot more 5,000 years ago than we know today.

Spirit Release with Irenka Danielewicz-Herbert
Thursday 9th July 2009

You know when you meet someone for the first time, and you just click? Or the opposite, you take an instant dislike to them? It could well be that you knew each other in a previous life, and you have brought with you the emotions, problems or preconceptions you felt back then.

Of course, if you don't believe in reincarnation (not everyone does), this may not be relevant to you. However, if you *do*, you should've been at our Slimbridge Dowsing Group talk by Irenka Danielewicz-Herbert on the subject of Spiritual Release Therapy on 9th July. Irenka explained in her strong Polish accent that we bring with us through many lifetimes old behaviours, patterns and programming, both good and bad.

We live our lives at three levels, says Irenka, the conscious mind, the subconscious mind and our Higher Selves. Our consciousness is subjective and judgemental, making decisions and choices, although not necessarily the right ones.

The subconscious is not judgemental, but constantly monitors and records everything it sees, hears, and learns, all thoughts, words and experiences, throughout many lifetimes. This may account for déja vu or any puzzling reactions, being your response to memories or events recorded in a previous life.

It also explains why you should speak gently and kindly to yourself, and avoid telling yourself you are stupid. Your subconscious will learn and remember that too, but isn't objective enough to disagree.

Interestingly, we seem to keep meeting up with the same people. Your husband or wife in this lifetime, may well have been your brother or sister, mother or father, in a previous one. This also applies to groups such as ours; Irenka dowsed and asked whether we had met before, and the unequivocal answer was yes, thousands of times!

The theory is that this happens because we come to this earth to learn lessons, choosing the lessons we need to learn. If we don't get things right first time around, we keep coming back, trying to fix things over and over again.

This is where the Therapy comes in. A trained and skilled therapist such as Irenka uses dowsing to research past life energies, subconscious blocks, and negative programming of the soul. Using a pendulum, a set of charts and a specific series of questions, discord can be identified and rectified.

We heard that thousands of people have been helped by Spiritual Release Therapy, and have gone on to live their lives more freely and joyfully, even becoming reunited with friends or family from whom they had earlier been estranged.

Slimbridge Horse Show – Saturday 25th July 2009

Slimbridge Horse Show was well attended and blessed with warm sunshine on Saturday 25th July, so we erected our gazebo and set out our stall in anticipation of a good day.

We were still glowing from our recent airing on BBC Radio Gloucestershire the preceding Monday and Tuesday, 20th and 21st July, when Faye Hatcher had interviewed our publicist, Trish Mills, and Chairman Peter Golding. Indeed, some visitors to our stall confirmed they had heard our interviews and enjoyed them, so they already knew a little more about dowsing than they had previously.

We didn't get to dowse or heal any horses, but Peter had great success with a lady's cat. She had brought along a photo of her pet specially and wanted healing for him. As always, Peter said, "Don't tell me what's wrong with him."

Peter works from several checklists – skeleton, nervous system, endocrine system, etc. With an eye on the photograph of the cat, and holding his pendulum in one hand, Peter ran a free finger down each checklist. It wasn't long before he announced, "Pancreas."

The lady looked startled, then beamed. "Yes!" she said incredulously. "That's right."

Peter then sent the cat absent healing.

"Hang on," said Peter, "there's something else here," and continued checking his lists. "There's something about this leg . . ." he said, peering at the photograph of the cat's face, but couldn't see anything untoward. "There's definitely something about this leg," he said, mystified, "but I can't find anything there."

"That's right," said the lady again. "That leg has been amputated!"

Health and Healing with Peter Golding
Thursday 13th August 2009

One of our members is seriously ill in hospital so, as part of his talk on Health and Healing on Thursday 13th August, Chairman Peter Golding taught us how to send him absent healing.

In preparation, however, he first took us through the process on a couple of volunteers from the audience, which included at least three or four interested new visitors who had either heard our recent interviews on BBC Radio Gloucester, seen the regular write-ups in the *Gazette* or simply found us on our website.

Using one dowsing rod, Peter held his free hand vertically, palm towards the volunteer, and asked to be shown the edge of their aura. One healthy lady had a good-sized aura, the second volunteer, a gentleman, had a significantly smaller one. This suggested some health problems, and Peter offered private healing afterwards, for which he does not charge.

Peter then demonstrated on a female volunteer that the first of the seven chakras, the head chakra, caused his pendulum to swing clockwise, the second chakra anti-clockwise, and so on. He then called upon a male volunteer, and showed that his first chakra caused the pendulum to swing the opposite way – anti-clockwise for the first, clockwise for the second, and so on.

This is how come male and female energy intertwines and works so well together, and how come male with male or female with female usually does not. There are exceptions to every rule!

Having introduced us to the aura and chakras, on another volunteer Peter asked to be shown the source of discomfort or malfunction, working down the body, across the body and the depth into the body. Once he had pinpointed the site, he used his checklists to establish exactly what the problem was.

He then asked the volunteer to turn her back to him, and dowsed the spine, asking to be shown where to send healing energy. When the pendulum reacted, Peter placed his middle finger on that spot, and envisaged white light or healing energy channelling through him. The pendulum went into overdrive, circling rapidly as the healing energy poured in.

Some people feel warmth or tingling as they are being healed. One gentleman said the pain had left his leg almost immediately, others can wait two or three days before they feel any benefit.

Moving on to the absent healing for our frail friend in Gloucester Royal, Peter handed round a photograph of him and emphasised that he had obtained permission for us to do this, which is important. Group energy can be very powerful and we hope it supported our absent friend and his wife in their hour of need.

Marine Archaeology – The Purton Hulks
Saturday 19th September 2009

We excelled ourselves at the Purton Hulks Open Day. We had been invited to dowse for hulks so covered in silt and sediment, they were no longer visible, and we found not one but several.

As local people are well aware, dozens of old boats have been intentionally beached along the eastern banks of the River Severn in order to prevent erosion. The idea, begun in 1909, has worked so well, many vessels have disappeared from view.

Historian and enthusiast Paul Barnett, founder of Friends of Purton (www.friendsofpurton.org.uk) reports that the Purton Ships' Graveyard currently numbers some 81 vessels, but there is plenty more to discover, which is where our dowsing rods came in.

There were six of us, and it was an exciting and challenging day. We were rewarded by dowsing and finding several scuppered vessels, all buried but some apparently on top of each other, one in particular dowsed as having been built in the 17th century.

We also found what we believed to be the prow of a ship, and wanted to know its length. Member Jon Martin, who is probably about 6ft, was particularly intrepid, and disappeared into a vast bed of reeds far taller than he was. He re-emerged, muddied but unbowed, thrilled to have found that on asking his rods for the location of rudder and stern, he had been led in a curve that coincided with the shape of the vessel. Further questions indicated that it had had three masts, was 100–115ft long, and probably had a 30–40ft long keel.

Our most exciting find of the day proved to be a buried rowing boat, dowsed by our Chairman, Peter Golding. He felt it to be some 33ft long, and 9ft wide, with no engine, no mast, and seats across it. We suspected this was a cutter that had been used to ferry goods and passengers from ship to shore, built in 1789.

When Paul Barnett came to see how we were getting on, he was delighted because he has records of just such a vessel but did not know where it was.

Peter Gibson, one of our most experienced archaeological dowsers, marked the outlines of the vessels with flags and yellow tape, and took GPS readings. "If it's worth dowsing," said Peter, "it's worth recording."

Obviously we did not excavate to confirm our dowsing predictions, but we are confident our results are accurate. We will give a plan of our findings and their locations to the Friends of Purton, and look forward to hearing how they compare with the findings of other archaeologists and 3-D radar imaging.

Sacred Geometry with Ced Jackson
Thursday 8th October 2009

Have you ever stopped to admire the shape of your credit card? It feels nice in the hand, doesn't it? Good proportions. There's not really any other shape it could be, is there?

According to Sacred Geometry, this shape is based on the Golden Section or Golden Mean, where the longer side is 1.618 times the shorter side. This is a sort of magic formula that can be applied to the shape of most rectangles, from football pitches to the building of a cathedral.

In his talk about Sacred Geometry on 8th October, Ced Jackson surprised us with just how much it applies to us and to every-day life. Consider the spiral staircase – one of the strongest designs there is. The spiral can be seen throughout the universe, from the shell of the worthy snail, the seeds in a sunflower, pine cones and even outer space. And there is a magic formula for that too.

Geometry is not just about formulae and codes, however. It literally means 'measuring the earth'. Many geometrical shapes have great significance, particularly the circle, which has long represented heaven and perfection.

If you place two circles so that they overlap, the shape you get common to both of them is a pointed oval, known as the *vesica pisces*. This sounds romantic until you learn it means 'bladder of a fish', but it too represents much of significance and lends itself to the design of cathedrals and even the Bishop's mitre.

Numerology gets in there too. Any size circle can be surrounded by a repeat of itself six times (try it with pennies), which gives us 6 + 1, another significant sum which might be why we are told God created the world in six days and on the seventh day He rested.

Our speaker lost us a couple of times but we persevered and learned the significance of squares too, which represent the earth. He's the only man we know that has ever made Pythagoras' theorem and the right-angled triangle even vaguely comprehensible. And then there's the pyramids . . .

The main gift our speaker brought us, however, was that we should look at things with new eyes, and realize there is a mathematical significance and an interconnectedness to all things, which applies in more ways than one to the humble credit card.

Christmas Party – Four more tables
Thursday 10th December 2009

A bit of continuity in these precarious times can be quite comforting and welcome. So this year we continued our ancient tradition (started last year) of having Four Tables for the Slimbridge Dowsing Group Christmas party.

No, this isn't so we all have lots of elbow room over the festive turkey, it's four tables with various items for us to try out our dowsing skills.

One member brought along three bottles of home-made wine and we had to dowse to see what it was made from (nettle, parsnip and gooseberries); how strong proof it was (a blistering 18–20%!); and what caused the cloudiness of the golden nectar?

The answer to this last was iron, because the wine-maker had collected pure (free) water from a Malvern well and it is rich in iron. Not many of us got that right.

Other tables included map dowsing to find several wells at Shepherds Patch; dowsing for faults in an electrical cable; and dating various items of pottery including a brick. Finally 'Remote Viewing' which is holding an envelope or package and seeing what your first thought is. None of us was very good at this, it takes practise, so maybe next year. (We said that last year!)

Continuity and tradition dictate that we'll all have another go at Christmas 2010, and that includes the glass of fizzy bubbly and festive nibbles afterwards.

Ann Lodygowski during her workshop on Thursday 9th June 2011.

Dowsing and Healing with Joey Korn on Thursday 19th April 2007.

Earth Energies with Dr Patrick MacManaway on 9th September 2010.

Dr Helen Ford, Perceiving Auras on Thursday 11th August 2011.

Emotional Freedom Technique with Diane Holliday on Thursday 14th April 2011.

Dowsing demonstration at the Dursley Festival on Sunday 13th July 2008.

Dowsing a photograph at Slimbridge Horse Show on Saturday 25th July 2009.

Reflexology with Isobel Willmott Saturday 25th April 2009.

Acupuncture with Dr Fiona Firth Thursday 11th November 2010. Ouch!

Map dowsing at the Four Tables Christmas Party 2009.

A visit to Avebury with Peter Golding and Isobel Willmott – 27th June 2009.

Dowsing at Avebury – 25th September 2010.

Avebury – 25th September 2010.

Photo: Peter Gibson

Secretary Barbara Davis and her daughter did us proud at the Flower Follies Festival in Slimbridge Parish Church on Bank Holiday Saturday 29th May 2010. She used delphiniums and white carnations to illustrate a fountain of water, and a spiral of yellow chrysanthemums to illustrate earth energies.

Sound Healing with Jan van der Elsen on Saturday 17th July 2010. On this occasion, Jan came to Slimbridge Village Hall, but later he also treated us to a sound healing bath on board Sula, *his refurbished lightship moored at Llanthony Quay, Gloucester Docks.*

Dowsing the Decagon with John Gibson-Forty, Thursday 13th May 2010. John spent three-and-a-half years dowsing the energy lines of a 4,000-year-old decagon (a ten-pointed, ten-sided figure) that stretches from Stafford in the north to Glastonbury in the south, and from Milton Keynes in the east to Llandovery in the west. It covers 22 counties and an area in excess of 14,000 square miles. Now that's a lot of dowsing.

The Healing Concept with Les Greve on Saturday 26th June 2010 – with banner.

Earth Energies and Leylines with Peter Gibson Thursday 11th January 2007.

Purton Hulks on Saturday 19th September 2009, and the dowsed outline of a lost ship.

Dowsing Thistledown with Barry Goldring on Saturday 23rd May 2009.

Ram Inn – most haunted – on Saturday 15th March 2008. When Arthur Marrow arranged for us to investigate psychic phenomena at the Ram Inn in Wotton-under-Edge, seventeen of us arrived with divining rods, pendulums and cameras at the ready.

This photograph of secretary Barbara Davis, and her late husband Colin, modelling our new tee-shirts, made the Gazette *on 25th June, 2009.*

Drilling proves a spectacular success after Peter dowsed Hurst Farm, Slimbridge.

Chairman Peter Golding, affectionately known as PG1, who started it all.

George Applegate, with Aaron Bray, Chairman of BSD Water & Site Dowsing Group and Peter Golding, Vice-Chairman of BSD WSDG, 25th June 2011. Photo: Patrick Callaghan

2010

Crystal Healing with Collette Stubbs
Saturday 30th January 2010

The comforting thing about crystal healing is that you can't overdose on it, you don't get unpleasant side effects and you can use several different crystals all at the same time.

In the western world we categorize this concept under myth and magic and therefore suspect. If we could only suspend our cynical disbelief, and trust and accept, we would learn so much.

When the speaker for our meeting on Saturday 30th January let us down literally at the last minute, we were understandably peeved. As it turned out, she did us a favour! The talk on Crystal Healing had been well publicised and members would have been disappointed to turn up and hear about water divining instead, so the hunt was on for another crystal healer who could step into the breach. Fortunately we found the perfect substitute in Collette Stubbs, who knows her stuff and showed us how to heal ourselves, rather than just telling us, which is always more exciting.

Crystals are given to us by nature, undoubtedly for our use. Depending on colour, size and structure, they are believed to help a variety of maladies from depression and bereavement to cramp and an increase in energy.

Collette invited us to rub our hands together, then, holding them slightly apart, to feel the resulting energy. She stood against a white board and suggested we look past her, rather in the manner of those magic 3D pictures, to see her aura. Some of us could, many of us couldn't. Not to worry, it will come.

We then dowsed the current size of our own auras and chose a crystal from a selection Collette had brought with her, all colours, shapes and sizes.

"You can either dowse for the best one for you with your pendulum," she explained, "or simply hold your open hand over the trays until your middle finger dips. If that doesn't work, just use your intuition and take the one that appeals to you."

If there's one thing you can trust in this world, it's your intuition. It instinctively knows what is best for your highest good and will never let you down. So, having chosen the best crystal for us, we measured again. Simply holding the small stone for a few moments changed the size of our auras!

Sometimes a crystal is for life, but often you only need it for a short time, until it has healed you. The best way to apply healing is by placing the relevant crystal on the appropriate chakra of the body – red, orange, yellow, green, blue, indigo, violet. Yes, the colours of the rainbow.

The other wonderful thing about crystals is the price. They range from just £1 for a tumbled stone while a bracelet can be as little as £2.99. That's cheaper than an NHS prescription!

Medicinal Herbs and Other Weeds with Ben Stiles
Thursday 11th February 2010

Ben Stiles is good value, not just as a speaker but also to the NHS – she must save them a fortune. Long before the drugs companies ruled the world, people still became ill, and still needed medication. They turned to the herbs, plants and weeds that grew naturally in their gardens and hedgerows, and those leaves, flowers and roots are just as efficacious today.

For her talk on 11th February, Ben from Ledbury had brought along a selection of plants that remain available during the winter months. Mostly indigenous to this country and therefore relatively hardy, mallow, comfrey and green alkanet are good for coughs, colds and sore throats. Herb Robert and elderberry leaves can be helpful too. Plantain, dock leaves, stinging nettles and dandelions are highly versatile and can help with a variety of maladies.

Ben is a living monument to the curative properties of many a plant. She claims foxgloves (digitalis) helped her heart condition, plantain stopped her nose bleeds (a symptom of high blood pressure), willow trees were the original – and natural – source of aspirin, and shepherd's purse cured her of just about everything else. She finds camomile calming, and the greater celandine is good for cataracts and glaucoma, applied in different ways.

You can use all the different parts of a plant, and apply it in teas, tinctures, warmed oils or simply a leaf dipped in cold water. Generally speaking, alpine plants and wild versions are more compact and therefore more concentrated than their larger cousins. Using the leaves, flowers, bark and roots, albeit in different forms and for different applications, makes for a good balance.

Ben warned that parts of some plants can be poisonous, for example mistletoe berries, but other parts of the same plant can be used to treat cancer and heart problems. Ragwort can be fatal for horses, it affects their liver; and some perfectly innocent plants such as St John's wort, gingko biloba and even garlic can cause problems if consumed while you are on Warfarin.

Ben is not above experimenting on herself but, unless you know what you are doing, don't try this at home! Either look it up in a good book or consult an expert on the subject. Either way, it's good value.

Rediscovering Avebury Henge with Maria Wheatley
Saturday 27th February 2010

OK, imagine you are a megalithic architect, it's about 3000 BC or earlier, and you've got all these henges to build. Stonehenge can wait, you must get Avebury done first.

You are more than aware of the earth's energies, magnetic flows and subtle geometry, and you have to mark these power centres with stone circles, protecting them with a ditch and a bank, and line it all up with sunrises and sunsets, the moon and certain stars. Accuracy is paramount.

You also realise your specialist knowledge will be lost over the centuries so it's vital to mark these important places. It will certainly give them something to dowse and wonder about in 5–6000 years time.

In her riveting talk on Saturday 27th February, Maria Wheatley from Marlborough, near Avebury in Wiltshire, explained in words and pictures the exciting discoveries she has been making by dowsing Avebury stone circle.

She has written a book on the subject and with co-author Busty Taylor, who is an archaeologist and pilot, has been able to view and photograph Avebury from the air. A bird's eye view is always an advantage and they could see patterns and alignments not evident at ground level.

Maria and Busty believe standing stones emit a form of energy, which can be readily detected by dowsing. The source of this energy is believed to be generated by the earth, absorbed by the standing stone and emitted through it. Many people claim they can feel this energy as a tingling sensation when they place their palms on a stone's energy-band.

Avebury has been much modified over the years, as farmers pulled down stones to smash up and use to build their own homes.

Some 200 years ago, someone erected a false bank which obstructed not only the view from the well-known stone, the Devil's Chair, but more importantly, the astronomical alignments too. Instead of the sunrise touching certain stones, this new bank left them in shadow. So much for modern man's so-called improvements!

Once again we were reminded just how much knowledge has been lost over the centuries, and how much we still have to learn and discover. Fortunately dedicated people such as Maria and Busty are on the case.

Herbal Medicine and the Heart Field with Nathan Hughes – Thursday 11th March 2010

Our speaker was surprised to discover a record turnout of 26 members for his talk titled Herbal Medicine and the Heart Field on the 11th March. We had had a fascinating talk on herbs and healing in February, but Nathan Hughes, an apothecary based at Ruskin Mill, Nailsworth, approaches the subject from a different direction.

"It's not simply about using herbs to treat dis-ease," he explained, and the hyphen is deliberate. "It's about restoring the wholeness of a person."

Herbs in this context means anything growing – trees, plants and weeds – that is used for medicinal purposes.

Early man, ancient tribes and even animals seem to have an affinity with them, instinctively drawn to the herbs and foods that can heal. A sort of inner dowsing, if you like, an ability we all have but have been talked out of over the centuries.

Nathan doesn't prescribe herbs for specific illnesses in the way your GP prescribes medication or drugs.

"Once the right herbs have been identified," he says, "it's more a question that we need to get out of the way, to allow healing to happen."

Most physical illnesses start with emotional trauma, which affects us mentally and spiritually, and later manifests in the body. It is therefore more important to identify – and treat – the cause rather than the effect.

This is why so many people are critical of western medicine which tends to treat symptoms and ignore the origin or cause of the problem.

Nathan can even home in on what part of the herb we need – leaves, bark, flower, petals, stamens, roots? And in what form to use it too – as a tea, a tincture, an oil, in a cream, as a salad, or even cooked?

He is convinced that herbs will be our salvation as so-called superbugs become more and more resistant to antibiotics. Man-made medication attacks the system with one hit, whereas herbs attack from seven or eight different directions at once. And more gently too, so that side effects are rare or less unpleasant.

Herbs are an antidote, not an antibiotic, and best of all, they can be found free of charge in your garden or in a woodland near you.

Practical Archaeological Dowsing with Peter Gibson
Saturday 24th April 2010

April's lovely spring weather found us dowsing for archaeology. At an earlier meeting we had learned the theory, and now we were keen to try it out in practice. It was exciting to know we could use our dowsing rods to discover different periods of occupation and that the depth at which artifacts were buried was no barrier.

Armed with dowsing rods, pendulums, surveying and recording equipment, including flags for marking the layout of buildings, a compass, measuring tapes and a global positioning receiver, twelve of us descended on two fields adjacent to member Peter Gibson's house in Shepherds Patch.

The house includes parts of two cottages built in the early 1800s, although an 1803 map of the Parish shows a building existing on that site by the 1700s. This is supported by artifacts found in the garden and a disused well, dated by the Gloucester Museum some 10 years ago and 'showing continuous domestic occupation since 1650'.

We have dowsed the property and surrounding fields on several occasions, and discovered many different occupation levels from pre-history onward.

In 2005 we confirmed that the original building had been a major farmhouse and the outline of the house and barn were traced. The top of the adjacent field had also been investigated, concentrating on the 16th-century occupation level, and a number of workers' cottages and pigsties were indicated.

This time we planned to home in on occupation during the 18th century. We divided into three groups, each led by an experienced dowser, and were allocated different sections of the field. The weather was perfect for field work, sun not too hot, no volcanic ash, and the ewes and lambs kept well away.

Several beginners were delighted with the quick response to their newly acquired skills. Asking our rods what was there in the 18th century only, it seemed several of the 16th-century buildings still remained, including that essential of any farming community, a cider and beer house. This genuinely was essential in those days because the water from relatively shallow wells would have been undrinkable.

Further dowsing indicated that the cottages had been demolished around the middle of the 18th century and a long hedge planted the length of the field.

Reference to the 1803 map, at first concealed from the dowsers, showed an orchard in that field, probably apples for cider. This could indicate a change of ownership or a reduction in the demand for wool.

Chairman Peter Golding marked the outline of a barn, 8 metres long by 4 metres wide in the field adjacent to the farmhouse.

Peter Gibson discovered a dwelling attached to the end of it; dowsing suggested it had been built around 1750 and demolished at the beginning of the 1800s, about the same time the canal was being built nearby. Other buildings in this field were probably demolished around the same time.

It's an ongoing labour of love to continue dowsing these fields in our spare time, and to develop the fascinating local history to be found there.

Dowsing the Decagon with John Gibson-Forty
Thursday 13th May 2010

Sometimes a subject is just too big for an hour's talk, and certainly too long to do it justice here. That was the problem facing John Gibson-Forty when he came to speak at our meeting on 13th May, but he held our interest and made us want to buy copies of his book, even though it isn't published yet.

John is an experienced dowser and has spent three-and-a-half years dowsing the energy lines of a 4,000-year-old decagon (a ten-pointed, ten-sided figure) that stretches from Stafford in the north to Glastonbury in the south, and from Milton Keynes in the east to Llandovery in the west. It covers 22 counties and an area in excess of 14,000 square miles. Now that's a lot of dowsing.

Centred on the tiny hamlet of Whiteleaved Oak, exactly where the three counties of Gloucestershire, Herefordshire and Worcestershire meet, the decagon sprouts ten energy lines like the spokes of a wheel, and of course an eleventh line forming the circumference.

Just to make things more interesting, John and his colleague, the late Peter Watson, soon discovered that dowsing these energy lines as they are today was no use, because they have changed, or moved, or suddenly ceased altogether. So they had to dowse them as they were in 2000 BC – 4000 years ago!

Each energy line incorporates various sacred buildings and sites, and naturally John had to dowse and research those too. Associated with King Arthur, the Knights Templar, other religions, and even sacred geometry, each line could fill a book all on its own.

But how did the decagon come to be there and what is its purpose? It is thought to be connected with the three perpetual choirs of Britain, each choir comprising 2,400 druids or monks who chanted on a rolling rota basis, 100 at a time, every hour of the day and night, in order to maintain the ongoing enchantment of Britain.

The first choir was based at Llantwit Major in South Wales, the second at Glastonbury, and the third at Amesbury, near Stonehenge. These three sites are to be found in the lower, western part of the decagon, and the ongoing chanting presumably influenced the whole area.

There is a second decagon, a comparable structure centred where the three counties of Cambridgeshire, Hertfordshire and Essex meet. But that's another story! It was difficult enough to cover one decagon in the time available, the second one will have to wait.

The Proof of the Dowsing is in the Drilling with Aaron Bray – Saturday 22nd May 2010

The better the weather the lower the turnout! Saturday 22nd May was glorious and our numbers suffered accordingly. It was a shame in a way because our speaker, Aaron Bray, a Cornishman who had escaped to Devon, was very interesting.

Aaron started life as a quarry engineer, with his brother inherited his father's rock drilling company, bought out the competition and a couple more drilling rigs, and now has 32 employees. He is one of the few drillers who is a dowser himself.

As dowsers, with a Chairman who still goes out to farmers, smallholders, garden centres, etc., to find the best spot for them to find an independent supply of water, it was fascinating to hear what happens after we've said, "OK, sink your borehole *here!*"

Aaron drills all over the country, and knows the geology of the southwest, the Channel Islands and Scotland like the back of his hand. In the southwest it's mostly hard rock, so he uses a 6-inch air rotary hammer drill, which pulps the rock as it sinks through it, and is then pumped out by air.

When you hit water, it can be quite spectacular since it is usually under pressure, and release can bring fountains 10 or 20 feet high. Then you have to dash for cover. Eventually it eases up and you can sink your 4-inch lining and your one-metre long, three-inch-diameter pump.

Before he gets that far, however, Aaron has to consider such variables as site access, weight and height restrictions, buildings, foundations, nearby burial sites, even hedges, which can be ancient, and even the neighbours, who are sensitive to noise.

Undergound pollution is a major consideration, as run off from pig sties, cowsheds and even the local graveyard, can affect the quality of the water.

Aaron's other preoccupation is, of course, cost. Insurance alone is £20,000 a year, plus labour, transporting the rig on a low loader, and massive amounts of diesel, all add up. His services can cost from £2,500 to £6,000 and in some cases £10,000, depending on depth. "The deepest I've drilled," said Aaron, "is 210 metres."

Once the borehole is finished, water often needs to be filtered, treated and stored. Depending on your source, you can expect between 2 and 60 gallons per minute.

At the end of the day though, however deep you drill, and regardless of cost, it is a fact that you can only take what water is there. So it is vitally important to find the right site to start with and Aaron is always worried until he gets that final confirmation that yes, we've found water.

Afterwards, we went to the fields across the road to practise water divining using the methods Aaron had described during his talk.

Flower Follies Festival, Slimbridge Parish Church Saturday 29th May 2010

We were delighted to be invited to take part in the Flower Follies Festival at the Parish Church, Slimbridge, over the May Bank Holiday weekend. It was special because historically the church had tried to stamp out dowsing and healing skills during the Middle Ages, and even today, some churchgoers are a little wary. Conversely, some of our members are regular churchgoers themselves!

So it was great to be welcomed and to add our display to others including Slimbridge's WI, Local History Society, Royal British Legion and Royal British

Legion Social Club, Horse Show, Horticultural Society, Twinning Society, Bright Lights Sunday School, Play Group, Variety Show Group (famed for their annual pantomime), the Parish Council, and a lovely white and gold wedding-themed history of the church itself in the Chancel.

Our Secretary, Barbara Davis, did us proud. She used blue delphiniums and white carnations to illustrate a fountain of water, standing on turquoise silk which looked watery too.

In our second windowsill, Barbara used a spiral of yellow chrysanthemums to illustrate earth energies, which often send our rods a-twirling.

There were also photo boards to show what else we get up to, and a small poster proclaiming Slimbridge Dowsing Group meetings when all aspects of dowsing – Water Divining, Health, Archaeology, and Earth Energies – are covered.

Dowsing Longbarrows at Coaley Peak with Jon Martin and Barbara Davis – Thursday 10th June 2010

If you've ever visited the Nympsfield longbarrow at Coaley Peak, you probably thought there wasn't a lot to see. A mound with a dent in the ground, some large stones and an information board giving a few details.

Yet when our dowsing group visited on Thursday 10th June, our rods indicated a great deal more, which was quite exciting. Our leader told us not to read the board before we began as that was cheating and might skew our results.

We began by asking when the longbarrow was built and all rods indicated 3200 BC, or 5,000 years old, which the information board confirms. Significantly it lies East West, facing the rising sun. Our rods indicated there were men, women and children buried there, but our numbers ranged from 12 to 17. The information board says 17.

Soon a couple of our members who are experts in this field began exploring the site and made some remarkable discoveries. Sacred places were usually built on rising ground and our rods indicated an avenue approaching the main entrance with five steps leading up to it.

Not far away we dowsed and found a round house (built 2300 BC) with a healing pit within it, where you could stand if you were sick or in pain, and your bad energy would go down into the earth. There was also a mortuary building and several ancient graves nearby so maybe this form of healing did not always work!

Having dowsed what had once been the physical, we moved on to earth energies, mainly spirals which usually appear in pairs and can be either beneficial or detrimental. A pair travels upwards, over and downwards and then back under to form a toroid or a bagel on it's side in a continuous movement, being energy. If you visit and start to feel nauseated, you are probably standing in a downward spiral. Move just a few feet away and you will immediately feel better.

Even the wild flowers in the meadow respond to spiral energy. Where we detected an upward spiral, the oxeye daisies were significantly larger, healthier and more prolific. Nature does know best.

The Healing Concept with Les Greve
Saturday 26th June 2010

"Look! Look!" someone cried in disbelief. One of our members has been hobbling around in severe discomfort for several years, and suddenly he was upright, raising his arms above his head, bending down to touch his toes, and beaming fit to burst.

What had happened? He had received healing from our speaker, Les Greve, on Saturday 26th June, and was about to throw away his walking stick.

At the start of his talk, Les told us these days you're not allowed to call yourself a healer, but people do tend to get better, so what else would you call it?

Les believes we create illness and dis-ease by our thoughts. They can establish themselves due to learned behaviour as a child or via vibrations perceived in the womb, and quoted several examples of patients he had been able to help. The more kindly a child is treated, and the more content and peaceful an expectant mother can remain, the better the child's future health will be.

Because we all consist of minuscule atoms of energy, Les' healing is done vibrationally. Consequently, he can send healing throughout the world, simply by hearing your voice on the telephone.

Love and intent is all, believes Les, and demonstrated his point with a volunteer. Using dowsing rods to show the original size of their aura, someone was then asked to say something unkind to the unsuspecting volunteer. His aura decreased dramatically. We then said something kind to the poor chap, and his aura reasserted itself. It is astonishing to discover we have such power over friends and loved ones – you truly should be careful what you say.

This healing ability only came to Les some five years ago, and he attributes it to a massive team of spirit guides who help him. His gift extends beyond people with physical illness and emotional distress; he has been able to revitalize an entire forest of dying trees and individual trees for the National Trust, as well as contaminated land, sick buildings and even ailing businesses.

It certainly worked before our very eyes for one of our members, who went home rejoicing and worried that his wife might be suspicious about what he had been up to.

Sound Healing with Jan van der Elsen
Saturday 17th July 2010

There are many different forms of healing, but they all have one thing in common. Unlike western medicine which concentrates on one symptom at a time, holistic healing therapies work by bringing the whole body into balance. Think of it as an orchestra that needs to be in harmony.

During his talk on Saturday 17th July, Jan van der Elsen said he in no way claims to be a healer, it is simply that various methods, and in this particular case, sound, stimulate the healing process.

Standing in front of an impressive display of Tibetan and crystal singing bowls, tuning forks and ancient drums, Jan said everything we hear has a considerable effect on us, which in turn generates thought and evokes memories. Loud, unpleasant sounds such as a siren or an explosion, trigger the 'fight or flight' reaction; whereas gentle, pleasant sounds, such as sweet music or birdsong on a spring morning, calms and relaxes us.

Everything is in vibration, and is therefore affected by other vibrations. Jan demonstrated this by pouring water into one of his ancient Tibetan singing bowls, and asking someone to dowse its energy. "Seven," said the dowser. Then Jan 'played' the bowl with a cushioned wooden hammer, and showed us the vibrations rippling through the water. When the volunteer dowsed it afterwards, its energy was 8.5. And when he dowsed as Jan was playing, it was 9.5!

Jan called for another volunteer and our dowser was asked to find the outer edge of his aura. Jan then used a different-shaped singing bowl, struck it so it began to hum and used it to brush the volunteer's aura for some minutes. When we measured his aura again, it had increased by an incredible three feet.

Running out of time, Jan played one of his drums which was mesmerising and pleasant. "Every culture has drums," said Jan, and reminded us of how tribal ceremonies can bring people into a state of trance.

"It's a very fundamental thing and releases the negative energies in your body. Even when you have hundreds of people drumming, they will always end up playing in rhythm together."

With his wife Agnes, Jan will soon be mooring his restored Lightship near Gloucester Docks, where they will offer a variety of therapies, including sound healing.

Purton Hulks Revisited
17th July 2010

During another Purton Hulks Open Day on Saturday 17th July, Paul Barnett challenged Slimbridge Dowsing Group members in front of a large group of visitors, asking them to dowse how many crew were on the 'Katherine Ellen' the day she was beached 58 years ago.

Dowsers had again been invited after their success last year at finding several hidden wrecks. Members Peter Gibson and Barry Goldring arrived early and attached the Group's new banner to a nearby hedgerow, always a challenge even in the slightest breeze.

They then got down to business and marked out the location of a couple of hidden hulks. Paul Barnett came along with the visitors, and invited Peter Gibson to explain his methods and how he had dowsed the outline of a hidden vessel. The visitors were fascinated.

Further along the path, Paul and the visitors came upon our Chairman Peter Golding, near the spot where he had previously identified the 'Katherine Ellen', a buried hulk whose location Paul Barnett was anxious to have confirmed. Peter showed the group how he dowsed the outline and walked round it following directions from his dowsing rods. They also indicated that the wreck was almost three feet below the existing surface.

Then Paul Barnett bowled Peter a googly! "In front of them all he asked me how many crew were on board the day she was beached. I needed a precise date for that, and Paul knew it – 7th August 1952."

As Peter was preparing to dowse, Paul whispered the answer to one of the lady visitors. Holding his rods – and his breath – Peter asked for the number of crew. "One? Two? Three?" and the rods crossed on three.

Paul asked the lady what he had whispered, and she said "Three." Records show that was indeed the number of crew the day the boat was run aground on the banks of the Severn. Said Peter, "They were amazed – and I was very relieved to have got it right!"

Slimbridge Horse Show – Saturday 31st July 2010

Dowsing can work in mysterious ways. On Saturday 31st July, we had our annual stand at Slimbridge Horse Show. Disappointingly we had few visitors, and the other stallholders were bemoaning the fact that there were very few people there this year.

The organiser of the event said the same when he paid us a courtesy visit. Many of us had put in a lot of work and expense preparing for the event. Such a shame we thought, until one member, Diane Holliday, said, "Let's dowse for them to come.".

With that she started spinning her pendulum and four people turned up straight away. Then a couple of others turned up to speak to us, view our displays and watch us demonstrating dowsing with rods.

Dowsers don't believe in coincidence so what other explanation could there be?

Animal Healing with Ann Lodygowski
Thursday 12th August 2010

Question: What do the following have in common? A reserved dog called Jemima, an unsociable cat called George, Flora the rabbit who is going into decline, and a horse with no name?

Answer: A piece of their hair or fur was dowsed by renowned animal healer Ann Lodygowski at our meeting on Thursday 12th August, who diagnosed their problems and prescribed which Bach flower remedy would help them best.

"This rabbit is constipated!" announced Ann, as her rods responded strongly to her many checklists.

"Yes!" agreed the flabbergasted owner, "she is!" Ann wanted to know why, and went through the possibilities. The rods indicated Yes to teeth.

"She's not chewing her food properly," said Ann, "that's what's causing the constipation." Back to the rods: "Upper left teeth? Bottom left? Bottom Right? Upper right?" Yes, said the rods again, upper right.

"She's biting her cheek and it hurts her."

The owner simply nodded in amazement.

"She does chew much slower than my other rabbits," he said, obviously wondering where you find a dentist for rabbits. "In the meantime," added Ann, "give her Slippery Elm. That will help the constipation."

George the unsociable cat was more of a mystery.

"Tell me how I can help you, George," commanded Ann, then reported, "He wants to go mousing!" The owner disagreed. "He doesn't like going out," she said.

"Why not?" said Ann, asking the cat, not the owner. "He's been attacked by another cat," she reported. "What colour? Black. He's been beaten up by a black cat. No wonder he won't go out!"

This could have happened because George wasn't feeling 100%. "What do you feed him on?" Dry cat food. "That can give them kidney stones," pronounced Ann, "or swollen kidneys. Add half a teaspoonful of sunflower oil to his food and make sure he has plenty of water."

Next! Ann was puzzled, there didn't seem to be anything wrong with Jemima, the reserved dog. The rods didn't respond very strongly to any of the checklists, although there was some suggestion of a stiff neck, a minor muscular problem on the left hand side. "She is very reserved, a bit of a mummy's girl, but she seems fine." The owner then revealed that Jemima had recently had two operations for cancer.

"Well she's fine now," promised Ann. "They got it all and she's going to be OK."

A lock of mane from the horse with no name prompted Ann to ask why no name. "It's from the horse of a friend of mine," said the lady who'd brought it. "She has two horses and I don't know if this is from Bas or Rosco." Ann's rods immediately divined this was mane from Bas.

And the Bach flower remedy needed was Vervain, which indicated he was wilful, fanatical or stressed. The rods said yes for stressed.

Dowsing via her checklists, Ann soon divined that he was shortsighted in his left eye. This meant he was spooked by what he thought must be dragons in the hedge on his left.

Further dowsing revealed several painful vertebrae. "You know the feeling," said Ann. "My back's killing me! His muscles tense up in response to the pain, and toxins congregate."

Poor old Bas also had problems with his large intestine. The peristaltic waves of muscular contractions weren't working properly, so he had a spastic colon which meant he was hungry, but too sore to digest his food properly, leading to colic.

Then Tommy, another cat, wouldn't reveal his age. Ann asked the owner how old he was. "I don't know," he said, "I had him from cat rescue." Back to her rods but still no answer. "Will you tell me your age, Tommy?" The rods banged backwards. An unequivocal NO! She soon worked out he was on a poor diet and recommended sardines, but then realised there was more to this than met the eye.

"What are his symptoms?" asked Ann, and the owner revealed that he suddenly sneezes or coughs and seems to have some sort of violent fit. By a process of elimination, Ann divined that Tommy was being affected by geopathic stress, negative energies that spiral naturally from the earth.

Envisaging the owner's flat, Ann's rods indicated that the problem was in a room on the left where there was a narrow detrimental energy line which, strangely, cats are drawn to and will sleep on. After a few moments of deep concentration on her rods, Ann announced, "I've just got rid of that negative energy line. It has gone."

Ann is very much in tune with the animal world, not just racehorses, which are her speciality, but with most animals, and humans too. Her general recommendation is to make sure they have at least some oil in their diets. And finally, if you see your dog eating grass, don't stop him.

Your dog knows what is best for him and the grass he needs contains vitamins, is a diuretic, an antibiotic and a spring tonic. It is soothing to his guts, the mucilage content lines the intestines and stomach, and it will help a urinary infection and constipation.

"But it makes him sick," you say.

That's because he has taken what he needs from it and will reject the rest. It's nature's natural medicine, says Ann, let him enjoy it. Animals can tell you what they need but it's easier with Ann.

Ley Hunting with Peter Gibson
Saturday 28th August 2010

Have you ever looked at a map and noticed that you could draw quite a long straight line joining up churches and even a cathedral along its length? The talk by Peter Gibson, our Vice Chairman, on 28th August, provided the answer. These are ley lines or, as they should more properly be called, leys.

Peter began by defining leys as track ways made by ancient man as he crossed the country for trade. To dowsers, they manifest as an alignment of sacred or secular lines in the landscape and can include fords and bridges, wells and ponds, the summit of hills, straight lanes and roads, castles, tumuli and longbarrows from prehistoric times.

Dowser and author Alfred Watkins (1855–1935) from Hereford, first coined the phrase after he saw that the countryside over which he had walked for many years, showed alignments with such frequency they could not be coincidental. So he dowsed and searched and came across old paved tracks, existing roads and sighting points such as stones and mounds. He called these alignments 'leys' and his book *The Old Straight Track*, published in 1925, is still the standard reference on the subject today.

To qualify as a ley there needs to be a minimum of five such features along a straight 25-mile line. Ley is an Anglo-Saxon word meaning pasture or clearing in the forest and is incorporated in many place names, notably Dursley, Uley and Coaley.

It is human nature to take the shortest route, and it was easiest for early man to journey in a straight line. He would choose a landmark such as the top of a hill or other prominent feature in the landscape, and go for it. On the way he would need to find water, and a safe place to rest.

Place names can often give an indication of the trade conducted there. Salt has always been a necessity and leys often pass through towns and villages such as Saltash, Whiteways, Whitsands and Wick. Similarly, Chip or variations thereof, i.e. Chippenham, indicate where flint tools were made by chipping away at pieces of flint. Examining maps and looking at place names can give the first indication of where a ley might be found.

Peter continued his talk by showing examples of where he had discovered leys in different parts of the county. Of particular interest was Tumpy Green Farm, (meaning a tump in a high place) where he traced an alignment from their garden (where dowsing indicates there was once a hospice and religious house), to Slimbridge Church, on to Hardwick and Quedgley, passing through Gloucester Cathedral and thence on to Leigh and beyond. In the opposite direction, the ley led to the church at Stone and beyond. We were able to follow this ley on the local OS map using rulers and a length of string.

To round off Peter's talk in Slimbridge Village Hall, the group went across the road to Slimbridge Church to dowse for any leys there. We were successful in finding two leys that ran right through the church, ˙ indicating how important the site was to early man, even before the present church was built in the 13th Century.

Earth Energies, Geopathic Stress and Agriculture with Dr Patrick MacManaway 9th September 2010
(Written by Barbara Davis)

How many of us say Grace or a word of thanks before we eat a meal these days? Dr Patrick MacManaway's talk on 9th September on earth energies, geopathic stress and agriculture gave compelling reasons why this custom, now usually forgotten, should be revived.

Dr MacManaway explained that there are subtle energies around us that are undetectable to the five human senses. Each of us has our own electromagnetic field, and our thoughts and intentions can affect other people and things even though we are unaware of it. So blessing food before we eat can improve its quality and render it more beneficial.

Ancient man was undoubtedly aware of these energies, and an aspect often overlooked by archaeologists and dowsers is that ancient sacred sites were erected by agricultural communities. Once ancient man settled down to clear land and begin farming in one place, these sacred sites were of great importance in improving crop yield.

It has been demonstrated in America that seeds taken to a stone circle, in which energy is focused, had a better rate of germination and grew more uniformly than other seeds. Yield increased by a staggering 300%.

Crops planted over stress lines created by underground water can suffer a 40% decrease in yield. Fruit trees are particularly sensitive; vegetables such as lentils, beans and cucumber are also affected although tomatoes are not.

Winter wheat planted in Perthshire in an energetically enhanced field yielded an extra 0.5 tonnes per acre and certain varieties of potato had an increased yield of 30%.

So there is little doubt that earth energies and geopathic stress can affect us and the crops we grow, and blessing our food with a grace before we eat it will make us truly thankful.

Avebury Stone Circle – A guided tour with Maria Wheatley – Saturday 25th September 2010

If you didn't have a watch, or the local church bell to chime the hours, how would you tell the time? Ancient man managed very well by tuning in to the sun, moon, planets and stars. He built many stone circles that tell not just the seasons, days and hours, but the precise minute the sun rises on certain dates. And, almost 5,000 years later, they remain accurate to this day.

The longest and shortest days (the solstices) fall on 21st June (longest day) and the 21st December (longest night). The equinoxes, when daylight and darkness are equal, fall on 21st March and 21st September.

Avebury Ring in Wiltshire, built some 5,000 years ago and older than Stonehenge, is a fine example. We visited on 25th September, the Saturday closest to the autumn equinox. Consequently there was a large number of pagans (worshippers of nature) in the stone circles which, although interesting to see, did prevent us from going to the very centre.

The day began with a tour of the stone circles, guided by Maria Wheatley and Busty Taylor, co-authors of the book, *Avebury, Sun, Moon and Earth*. Using her dowsing rods, Maria indicated the seven energy bands on the large stones and their alignment with the sunrise and sunset of the winter solstice.

She also explained the interaction of the famous Michael and Mary ley energy lines as they traverse the country from Cornwall to Norfolk, intertwining like serpents.

We were amazed at how, five thousand years ago, they managed to transport such huge stones, and dig holes over 11 feet deep to set them in position. It is calculated that there were between 500 and 600 stones when the circles were complete, surrounded by a deep ditch and high bank.

Over lunch discussion continued as to dowsing techniques and what we were going to look for during the afternoon. We began with a visit to the Church where we detected four ley lines and strong energies coming from the font.

Finally we spent time amid the remains of the northern inner stone circle, investigating the double spiral energies around the huge sarsen stones and finding that, as Maria had said, the spiral energies reversed direction. One member found a slim cone of energy on the Mary line that seemed to be the trigger for this reversal.

OK, telling the time is easier with a digital gold Rolex, but not half as interesting.

Dowsing in Woodchester Park with Barry Goldring
Thursday 14th October 2010

Our leader, Barry Goldring, has done dowsing surveys for the National Trust in the past, and on Thursday 14th October he took a group of us to visit the terraced garden in Woodchester Park, courtesy of the Trust.

Barry and another member had surveyed and dowsed this nineteenth-century garden a few years ago, but he wanted to fill in more of the details to help the warden, Michelle Oliver, plan the next stage in its development.

Seven dowsers and five newcomers turned up, so we included some training into our visit. Peter Gibson led a group to get some more detail on the summer-house ruin, originally a stone building in the form of a Greek temple. The rods indicated a pair of stone lion-like beasts on plinths flanking the summer-house, and a walled area with square flower and herb beds in front of it.

One of our newcomers said she could feel warmth where she had been standing, and this was found to be one of a line of energy spirals located down one side of the walled area.

Further down the garden, other members dowsed the site of a rectangular paved area that had previously been something of a mystery – what had it been used for? The usual garden features – statue, urn, seat – produced no response from our rods, but further dowsing indicated that it had been a stone sculpture, possibly of part of a tree, that could be used as a seat but not originally intended for that purpose. This needs more investigation.

Too soon we were out of time, and were grateful for a lift back to the car park in the National Trust minibus.

Reflexology Healing with Avril Holland
Saturday 23rd October 2010

Have you ever wondered why babies and puppies always put everything in their mouths? The lips are probably our most sensitive form of sensor as they have the most nerve endings, literally thousands of them. This is followed by the fingertips and, not mentioning the naughty bits in between (this is a family publication), the soles of the feet and toes come third.

So no, we didn't have to take our shoes and socks off for the reflexology demonstration with Avril Holland on 23rd October, because we were able to do it on our hands instead. Very handy!

Both the feet and hands replicate the body, with meridians that correspond to various organs and areas.

By creeping your thumb caterpillar-style over the appropriate contact point on either, you can relieve various conditions and symptoms.

If you have a serious problem with a given part of the body, you can often feel a crystal build-up of toxins in the corresponding area of the hands or feet. Breaking it down can be quite painful, but once achieved, drink lots of water to flush the toxins away, and you will find the original problem is considerably relieved. Better still, a qualified practitioner will do it for you.

As with all these alternative and complementary healing therapies, the main objective is to bring the body into balance and harmony, and reflexology can support patients with a variety of ailments, from sinus to heart problems.

AGM and Acupuncture with Dr Fiona Firth
Thursday 11th November 2010

Doesn't it amaze you that something understood and accepted by the Chinese for thousands of years, has now been proved to work by sceptical westerners and is available on the NHS?

Acupuncture has been utilised in the Far East for over five thousand years. They knew even then that 'chi' (that's energy to you and me) flows through the body, and if it becomes blocked or out of balance for any reason, health problems ensue.

Maintaining a balance within the body was their priority, and their diagnostic 'tools' were simply looking at the tongue and taking your pulses. Yes, pulses plural, we have at least five, each representing one of the elements – wood, fire, earth, metal and water. And the tongue can tell us a lot about a patient, but not just verbally. Colour and coating are great giveaways.

Treatment is by simple needles, inserted into the appropriate spot in order to allow the chi to flow and the body to balance itself naturally. Regular and frequent acupuncture to balance the body and mind enabled the Chinese to stay healthy, prevention being better than cure. Whereas we wait until things have gone badly wrong and try to fix it afterwards.

The exciting thing is, said Dr Fiona Firth in her talk following our AGM on 11th November, that we are now able to prove acupuncture works to the extent that it is available on the NHS.

Tests have shown that if a qualified practitioner inserts the right needles into the right acupuncture spots on the right meridians (energy lines), the effect on the brain will show up on an MRI scan. Well, you can't argue with that, can you?

Obviously acupuncture is better at treating some things than others. Pain control to the extent that a willing patient can cheerfully have a tooth removed with just a couple of needles in place is more than impressive. Backs. Knees. Asthma. Menopause. Digestive complaints. It is apparently fantastic for gynaecological problems including female infertility, but every acupuncturist dreads being asked to treat tennis elbow! It doesn't seem to work for tennis elbow, maybe because we exhaust all other avenues first and only turn to acupuncture too late in the day.

If you've ever resorted to one of those wrist bands to alleviate travel sickness, you have already used pressure acupuncture. The vital thing is to hit the right spot. About two thirds of the population feel the benefit of acupuncture, and a third do not.

Interestingly, this mirrors the general response to morphine. Two thirds of us respond well, but a third are low morphine responders and do not experience the same level of pain relief.

There are 14 meridians throughout the body and some 370 acupuncture spots, so it takes some training and application to learn all that. A trained practitioner will be able to 'feel' the right spot to insert his or her needles, and feel a difference in the skin. Equally, she will know the right time to pull the needle out! Too soon and it won't want to come. As this can vary from 30 seconds to thirty minutes, it is a skilled assessment indeed. Fiona demonstrated on volunteer Peter Golding. His comment? "Ouch!"

As we know, doctors are not allowed to treat animals but qualified vets are also using acupuncture more and more. An animal naturally knows when you are trying to do it good.

For those who can't face 'the needle', there are alternatives in electronic and laser devices which is effectively acupressure and does not hurt at all. Our speaker admitted though that results might not necessarily be quite as good.

During a lively question and answer time, members asked if Fiona had tried reflexology and Reiki. Indeed she had, and dowsing too. "It's all rivers running into the same sea," she said. "Anything that unblocks the flow of energy and balances the body not only works, but today it is seen to work too."

A Labyrinth in Troytown with Peter Golding
Saturday 27th November 2010

Question: What is the difference between a labyrinth and a maze?

Answer: A maze is for fun, a game with lots of pathways and blind alleys for getting lost in, whereas a labyrinth is a spiritual experience with one pathway in and one pathway out, and can help you find yourself.

Before about 1400 BC, in Greek mythology, Daedalus built a labyrinth/maze in which to hold the Minotaur, a creature that was half man and half bull. Many forms of the labyrinth appeared in ancient Greece, Egypt and other parts of the world.

Excitingly, we have one locally, in Troytown near Slimbridge. The name, which seems to have roots in Greek mythology, alerted our speaker and Chairman, Peter Golding, to its existence some years ago, as the word 'Troy' in a place name usually means there was or is a turf maze or labyrinth to be found there.

On investigation, there was no physical evidence of anything whatsoever, but by map dowsing with his pendulum, Peter established its position in a field beside ancient footpaths. He then visited the site with his dowsing rods and discovered that the energy was still very much in evidence. His rods indicated that this labyrinth was last used in the 1920s and was probably first placed there in the 1500s.

Peter was so excited by his discovery, he was invited to talk about it to the Slimbridge Local History Society in March 2003. As a direct result of that meeting, a number of attendees wanted to learn how to dowse, and the Slimbridge Dowsing Group was formed the following June. It began with just eight people and we now have almost 40 members.

Originally the labyrinthine shape would have been laid out on the ground with turf or stones. If you walk a path through the seven circuits leading in, meditating as you go, reaching the centre can be a truly uplifting experience. You then leave by the same seven pathways and as you exit, you turn and give thanks, even though you may not know to whom.

This energy still works to this day and enthusiasts can build their own labyrinth in the garden; one was seen at the Spring Gardening Show at Malvern's Three Counties Showground recently.

Dowsing indicates there is frequently water below the centre, but this may well be mere resonance, and not water at all. It also appears to be of 100% purity, which qualifies it as holy water. Severn Trent please take note!

Various theories for its original purpose have been put forward. The focused energy seems to provide the spiritually uplifting experience of sacred space.

Another possibility is that people may have placed their grain and seeds in the centre in order to improve crop yield when planted. This has been proved to work in the 21st century, and in pyramids as well.

Our forebears were highly preoccupied with sacred geometry, and Chartres Cathedral in France has a magnificent labyrinth dating from about AD 1225, a copy of which appears in Gloucester Cathedral annually. Why not visit next time it appears? Enjoy the experience which, we are confident, will simply raise more questions than answers.

2011

Forum on Dowsing Questioning Skills with our three wise men, Peter Golding, Peter Gibson and Barry Goldring – Thursday 13th January 2011

Even the very best of speakers is nothing and nobody without a good responsive audience. Our first meeting of the new year on 13th January was a forum on how to phrase your questions clearly when dowsing. And we now have so much expertise and experience within our ranks that the excellent turnout meant the lively audience contributed almost as much from the floor as the three wise men at the top table.

Chairman Peter Golding gave the introduction, saying our rods can only answer Yes or No, or indicate a direction such as due north, so it is imperative to phrase our questions succinctly and be very specific.

We should always begin by asking, "Please may I dowse? Am I ready to dowse? Should I dowse?" If the dowsing rods move in the No direction to any of these questions, you should wait a while, rest, and drink some water before trying again. "You have to centre yourself," said Peter, "and feel calm within."

Sometimes it's just not appropriate to dowse at all, the rods will tell you.

Once you've received the OK, you need to protect yourself. If you are offering healing to someone, or could be exposed to bad energy, this is important.

Our three wise men, Peter Golding, Peter Gibson and Barry Goldring, each revealed their techniques for such protection, which relies on visualisation – usually envisaging a cloak of blue or white light or a shield of shining silver surrounding you.

Sometimes our questions are limited by our own lack of knowledge. One lady in the audience reported asking her rods what a ruined building had been built of – bricks? stone? wood? No, no and no. What else was there? Someone then suggested cob – clay and straw used as an ancient building material, of which she had never heard. The answer was Yes.

Another lady recommended being very wary of left and right. "I once surprised a gentleman by telling him he had a bad knee, which was correct. But then I asked my rods whether it was right or left, but didn't make it clear whether I meant *his* right or left or *my* right or left. I was facing him, so it made a difference."

Someone else reported searching for a friend's missing car keys. "My pendulum kept answering Yes to several places, which was very confusing," she said.

This was quickly diagnosed by everyone in general as 'remanence', a residual energy. The keys had been in all those places, and the rods could detect this. The question should have been "Where are the missing car keys NOW?"

Dating things can be a minefield. If you ask how old a clay pot is, your rods might indicate that it is millions of years old because the clay itself could be that ancient. You need to ask, "When was this pot made?"

In archaeological dowsing, it's best not to ask, "How old is this wall?" because the stones might have been used in a previous building elsewhere. You need to say, "When was this wall first constructed?"

You also need to be wary of preconceived ideas. Dowsers will frequently say, "Don't tell me anything about it!" so that they can approach with an open mind. If someone asks you to find their missing purse, and says, "I'm pretty sure it's in the kitchen," you've been pre-programmed, and your rods will often agree it's in the kitchen, even if it isn't!

Wise man Peter Gibson has a particular interest in earth energies and mentioned finding leys and ley lines, because if that's all he asks for, he sometimes gets an energy line instead. "I make it very clear," he said, "and describe a ley, which is the route taken by many people in the past. Usually a trade route or a path for pilgrims." This again is remanence.

Wise man Peter Golding, a water diviner for many years, said his most frequently asked question from farmers and gardeners hoping he will find a place for them to sink a borehole, is "How much water will I get? What will be the flow rate?"

This is another minefield, and Peter is always careful to ask his rods for gallons per minute through a given pipe width and from a certain depth in both wet and dry seasons. Such factors can vary flow rates considerably.

A gentleman in the audience asked if he could use dowsing to discover the best place to buy a house.

Wise man Barry Goldring said sometimes Cosmic Ordering works better than dowsing. "Put out to the universe what you want – the sort of home, area, price, etc., that is suitable for you, and then put it out of your mind. It will come to you when the time is right."

It's not what you say, it's how you say it.

Earth Energies with Jon Martin
Saturday 22nd January 2011

Dogs and cats are wiser than we are. They remain in touch with their instincts, whereas we, with our higher intelligence and sophisticated education, have never been so out of touch with ours.

Animals and even plants are very sensitive to earth energies. The energy emanating from the earth's molten core resonates at 7.83 Hertz, as does the human brain when we are relaxed or in meditation. When we get stressed or angry, that resonance changes, and we are immediately out of sync with our environment.

This oscillation is so important to our wellbeing, NASA had to reproduce it artificially in spacecraft because their astronauts became quite ill without it.

The earth's resonance changes in places, affected by something as apparently innocent as an underground stream, mineral deposits or other natural phenomena. This will mean parts of our host planet are out of harmony with us. Such negative energy is referred to as geopathic stress, which can disrupt the harmonic sequence and affect not just the human body but our auras as well, where most illnesses begin.

Energy spirals and ley lines can affect us too, as well as the oscillations from many of our electronic devices today, particularly mobile phones.

Dogs don't like geopathic stress and will avoid such areas. If a dog's bed is inadvertently placed on or near negative earth energy, the dog will become ill. Whereas cats positively seek it out, revel in it, and will return to a favourite spot time and again.

Having got us really worried, our speaker, Jon Martin, asked for a volunteer to demonstrate this effect. We've known for sometime that there is a geopathic stress line running through Slimbridge Village Hall, so Jon chose someone who happened to have been sitting in it – in the front row! Jon then did some muscle testing (kinesiology) and found the muscles had certainly been affected.

Another volunteer dowsed his aura, and found it to be a mere five feet.

Standing well away from the stress line, Jon then sought to heal the aura of the brave volunteer, taking a few moments to send healing with intent. The aura was then dowsed again and had increased to almost seven feet, and the volunteer agreed he did feel significantly better.

Asked how he sent such healing, Jon replied that he concentrated on the same meridians running through the body that are accessed and treated by acupuncturists, which has been proved to work. Then he simply sends good energy with the intent to heal.

Prevention is always better than cure, and many

cultures solve the problem by not building over areas of geopathic stress. The Chinese orientate buildings to avoid it, the Aborigines refer to it as song lines, the Irish have their fairy lines, they all respect such phenomena but we Brits refuse to believe any of it and build all over it – with inevitable results!

Clues as to whether you have geopathic stress in your garden or home can be found by observing where the cat has a favourite spot, where the dog refuses to go or even by observing plants in the garden, where some will grow bigger than others.

Getting to Know You – Thursday 10th March 2011

We have such interesting speakers and are so fascinated by dowsing, we sometimes forget to take an interest in each other. So Thursday 10th March was the day we actually listened to other members' dowsing experiences.

Trish Mills kicked off by telling us about her 2010 visit to Newgrange, the finest of many passage tombs just north of Dublin in Ireland, and the spirals she found there. Newgrange was built in 3200 BC so is over 5000 years old. It pre-dates similar passage tombs in Orkney, is 1,000 years older than Stonehenge and even pre-dates the pyramids, built some 700 years later.

The most important feature of Newgrange is that it is astronomically aligned. It has a roof-box above the entrance through which the sun lights up the entire length of the 60ft long passage every 21st December, the winter solstice.

Trish was much struck by all the megalithic art on the stones at Newgrange, spirals, rectangles and lozenges (diamonds) which obviously had great significance for these people. Which came first? Did they build on that site because they found energy spirals there in the first place, or did the energy spirals come after the sacred site was created?

For spirals there are in plenty. At the entrance, Trish reported holding up her rods as they sailed round and round at great speed. It was uplifting and extremely positive energy. However, having walked the 60ft long passage into the central cruciform (cross-shaped) chamber, she held up her rods again and they spiralled in the opposite direction. This meant negative energy, and Trish reported feeling extremely nauseated, and as if she was being pushed over. It lasted for some time, and when she mentioned it to the guide later, he said a lot of people reported the same sensation.

After that, other members were emboldened to share their dowsing experiences too. Ann modestly revealed that she has been offering healing to people and animals for some time. Patrick had dowsed to find out which supplements he needed, and used map dowsing to discover the best area in which to buy a house.

While some folks prefer rods, Jim is a whiz with his pendulum, and used it to find out why he kept waking up at night, and lying awake for hours, unable to get back to sleep. After excluding just about everything, Jim's pendulum indicated the problem was electricity entering the house. So he placed a cluster of crystals over the fuse box, and now sleeps better than he has for years.

Mary has an engineering background and confessed to being a little bit sceptical about dowsing – until she joined us dowsing at the Patch near Slimbridge one day and her rods indicated a pigsty. When she turned out to be right, she was thrilled, and went on to dowse Kingswood Abbey and found a priest hole.

Keith has been coming to SDG meetings for four or five months and still can't do it yet. Everyone assured him he will eventually, and to keep trying.

Sue had been unwell for some time and although on the mend, was still feeling vulnerable. She found there was "so much coming in", almost overwhelming her, but she enjoyed the meetings, particularly John Gibson-Forty's talk about dowsing the Decagon and the Perpetual Choirs, active in Druid times.

Vice-Chairman Peter Gibson, affectionately known as PG2 and one of our most experienced dowsers, sportingly reported a rare failure, the most fascinating case of remanence ever.

He had been asked to dowse for an aircraft that had crashed during the war. He located the remains of the plane by map dowsing, got permission to access the land, and had soon dowsed the outline and wing of a Hurricane. He found the engine, a B12 Merlin, which had broken into two pieces; located the machine guns and even found the propeller – behind the plane, not in front, obviously the first thing to hit. Yes, this was definitely it.

So they wheeled out the metal detectorists and a WW2 Bomb Disposal squad and started digging. Peter was confident it was some 30 feet down.

Imagine his distress and embarrassment when, after considerable excavation, there was nothing there! Distraught at the thought of the loss of not only his own reputation but that of dowsing itself, Peter dowsed again and phrased the question he should have asked in the first place. "Is it there NOW?" His rods whisked outwards, No! "Had it been there?" Yes! "When was it removed?" 1948. Exit Peter, another lesson learned, this time the hard way!

Then we moved on to Maureen, who said she had just started the journey, but was mainly interested in health, and had just been on a BSD Basic Dowsing and Health course.

Jon has been dowsing for two to two-and-a-half years, and his special interest is earth energies and the electromagnetic field. He had recently had the privilege of 'healing' several dogs belonging to friends; two greyhounds and a Rottweiler, all of which were well loved, well looked after, but mysteriously ill. Jon dowsed and noticed that the baskets in which they slept were on negative energy lines or being affected by electromagnetic fields. He was proved right, and suggested the dogs' beds be moved to a new site. This was done and the dogs are now fully recovered and in rude health. Impressive! Well done, Jon.

Frank followed, and has been a member for over two years. He enjoys the meetings because we are a group of such lovely people! He gets a strong reaction when he dowses but isn't very confident about what he finds. He had some success on our trip to Thistledown, found spirals and the site of a fatal crash in the 1920s when two people died; not sure if it was an aircraft or a hot-air balloon. On a second visit he went the wrong way and accidentally found the site of some buried treasure! The rods indicated it was buried about 5 feet deep, and Frank says one day he will go back with a spade to see if he was right or not.

Mike is fascinated by crystals and crystal healing, and stands them in the moonlight for cleansing. He is also fascinated by how dowsing works and suspects the pineal gland, and the remnant of our third 'vestigial' eye. He thinks he may have found a longbarrow in Cheltenham and wants more practise.

Another Mike had just come along for the first time and was thrilled – and relieved – to find so many like-minded people.

Diane is a kinesiologist and nutritionist, and taught herself dowsing twenty years ago. She dowses to find out which supplements her patients need, but otherwise says she does not use it enough.

Barbara comes from farming stock and once used dowsing to find out which ewes were pregnant after a ram got into their field. She had a good success rate but later, when she was told she was to become a grandmother, she dowsed her daughter and said it would be a boy. Barbara is now the proud grandmother of a beautiful baby girl!

Peter our Chairman ended the session by describing a day in the life of a water diviner. He has been doing this for over thirty years, but more recently he has become interested in dowsing for geopathic stress, health and healing.

It just goes to show how many applications dowsing can be used for, and the wonderfully interesting people it attracts.

Dowsing in Time with Barry Goldring
Saturday 26th March 2011

Do you remember that terrible accident on the 5th November 2010 when a ready-mix concrete lorry drove off a bridge near Oxshott in Surrey, and landed on a passing train on the railway tracks below?

Our speaker on 26th March 2011, Barry Goldring, remembers it well because he had had an accident at that precise location himself, twenty years previously. Nothing as dramatic, thank goodness, but last November's tragedy reminded him, and set him wondering why?

Was there a detrimental energy ley at that spot? His rods said No. But then he dowsed again, and asked was there a detrimental energy ley there at the time of the major accident? Yes! And had there been a detrimental energy ley there at the time of his own minor accident 20 years previously? Yes again!

Barry went on to say this concept of time was highly applicable to archaeological dowsing. He often found he received different answers to the same question, and had come to realize both were correct, but in different time zones.

He mentioned a local farm in South Gloucestershire where he had been asked to dowse, and discovered a large building but of a very strange shape. Walls seemed to come and go at random. After some confusion, it transpired there had been five buildings on that site over the years.

All he had to do was pick one part of a wall – any wall! – and dowse a date for it. Then he could continue asking for the outline of the wall for that date only. "And when you are asking," said Barry, "don't assume saying the date once is enough. Keep repeating the question and the date."

On a greater scale, this concept can also be applied to dating astronomically aligned monuments such as Avebury, Stonehenge, etc. Because of the way the earth has moved on its own axis during the last millennia, today the sun, moon, planets and stars rise and set at an altered angle of some 18 degrees.

This applies to leylines too, so when he was dowsing Coaley Peak longbarrow, Barry asked not for the leyline, but where the leyline had been when the longbarrow was first built. It was most satisfying to discover a disparity of 18 degrees.

Emotional Freedom Technique with Diane Holliday
Thursday 14th April 2011

Tapping is the new acupuncture. Known as Emotional Freedom Technique (EFT), it works in the same way as acupuncture, by unblocking the meridians or energy pathways throughout the body. The nice thing is though, no uncomfortable needles and, best of all, you can do it yourself.

The speaker at our meeting on 14th April, Diane Holliday, an advanced EFT practitioner and professionally trained in a variety of alternative and holistic therapies, explained that everything is interconnected. The root of any negative emotion is a disruption in the body's energy system. This leads to stress, which manifests itself as disease, illness, anxiety, phobias and addictions.

Acupuncture is a physical way of unblocking the meridians, but EFT combines physical tapping with conscious thought and the power of the mind. You simply need to concentrate on your current problem, issue or source of pain, and repeat certain mantras as you tap with your index and middle fingers on points around the eyes, the mouth, and under the arm at bra strap level. "I know the men don't wear bras," admitted Diane cheerfully, "but they know where that is!"

Diane then led us through the mantras, repeating out loud together: "Even though I have this 'issue' I completely accept myself, without judgement."

Then move on and say out loud, "Even though I hate having this feeling of anger/guilt/negativity/phobia, I absolutely love myself." And finally, "Even though I can't stop smoking/drinking/over-eating, I totally forgive myself."

Yes, you'll feel silly to start with, everyone does, but it is highly therapeutic, has no bad side effects and can genuinely work for you. It can also work for children and animals; Diane usually does this using a surrogate teddy bear or fluffy dog, repeating the mantras while tapping the relevant acupuncture points on their fur. The children love it.

The day after Diane's talk, I met a friend in the supermarket who had been there too, and we both agreed we'd had the best night's sleep in a long time.

Sound Healing Bath with Jan van der Elsen
Thursday 12th May 2011

To be bathed in sound can be so healing, and a route into deep meditation at the same time. It has to be the right sort of sound though – drums, Tibetan singing bowls and magnificent larger vessels made from quartz crystal are best.

Our sound bath on Thursday, 12th May was presented by Jan van der Elsen on board the lightship *Sula*, moored at Llanthony Quay just south of Gloucester Docks.

Jan and his wife Agnes also used seeds inside a bamboo casing that sounded like wind in the trees, and other instruments including a huge Indonesian gong, Shamanic drums, Tuning Forks, bell strings and rattles.

Played harmoniously to members and guests, we all agreed it was the most soothing, calming experience.

"Absolutely everything is in vibration," explains Jan, owner of the lightship, "including our bodies. The brain's normal vibration frequency is 13 to 16 or 17 Hertz (Hz). Below that, 13 down to 8 Hz, you are in the Alpha state, getting into meditation and deep relaxation."

Below 8 Hz, of course, you are asleep. At the other end of the scale, someone who is hyper, in a panic or even in a fight-or-flight situation, will have a brain vibration of 17 to 20 Hz, best avoided.

If you envisage your body as being an orchestra, it follows that if any part of it goes wrong, the whole thing needs re-tuning. As the famous playwright William Congreve said, 'Music hath charms to soothe a savage breast', and it does have a calming influence, although of course some modern music can have the opposite effect!

"The singing bowls in particular," continues Jan, "have been made for centuries by Tibetan monks as a tool to lower brain frequency to about 9 Hz. They worked an alloy comprised of seven to ten different metals, to produce the special sound that worked for them, and sent them into meditation, which was an important part of their daily lives."

After the wonderful experience of the healing sound bath on historic *Sula*, those present were persuaded that maybe meditation should be a part of our lives too.

Archaeological dowsing on Cam Peak with Peter Gibson – Saturday 28th May 2011

A housing estate on Cam Peak car park? Well, not today, no, but there used to be – four and five thousand years ago.

When fifteen of us went to dowse Cam Peak on a very windy, cold and rain-threatening Saturday 28th May, our archaeology enthusiast Peter Gibson set us searching for possible roundhouses dating back to pre-history times, before the Romans came to Britain in AD 45.

Peter had visited Cam Peak on a previous occasion and his dowsing rods had indicated a longbarrow. Today it was roundhouses, and dividing members into three groups, each led by an experienced dowser, proved fruitful indeed.

We dowsed several circles in a small area, which indicated buildings built on the same spot at different times over the centuries. Members then chose different areas to mark the outline of a wall, either built of stone, about a metre high to support the roof timbers and a thatched roof, or made of wattle and daube with the roof timbers set in post holes in the ground.

The access door and central hearth were then dowsed for too, and both inside and outside dowsed for storage pits dug out of the ground, for keeping food and grain during the winter. The whole community would have had to be self-supporting in every way.

There were also two extremely large roundhouses, 13–14m in diameter, which could have been meeting houses or large homes for several families. The entrance was facing east, away from the westerly wind and weather, and possibly to catch the rising sun at the summer equinox or to observe the rising planets.

All too soon, the rain came down to close the training session but we plan to return to Cam Peak to see what else we can find. "It is a sacred area," said Peter, "you can feel it."

Animal Healing Workshop with Ann Lodygowski Thursday 9th June 2011

Folks were queuing to get in to the meeting on Thursday 9th June. Forty people keen to hear Ann Lodygowski, renowned animal healer, communicator and amazing lady, who certainly pulls in the crowds.

Most attendees had brought a 'witness', samples of hair from their horse or pet, and we were shown how to determine ailments or dietary deficiencies in the animal by holding the witness and watching the reaction of our dowsing rods or pendulum while we scanned checklists of various health problems.

Ann told us of one recent healing where she thought she had lost the plot. A horse was refusing to go into its stable, it was thoroughly spooked, but there was no apparent reason for this behaviour.

"I kept getting the image of a highwayman," she said. She even asked a dowsing friend to check too, and he said the same.

In some trepidation, Ann told the owner, who calmly said, "Yes, that makes sense. This house is very old and a famous highwayman used to live here."

The horse was being spooked by a ghost! Ann asked the ghost to go to the light, to leave and be happy, and the horse has been fine in its stable ever since.

Ann then went on to spook her audience by telling us all the horrors to be found in some pet foods. She asked us to consider carefully what we feed our pets, and make sure they get a balanced diet.

"You can dowse for this too," she said, and gave out further checklists so that we could ask if he/she was healthy physically, mentally and emotionally, and check for such things as amino acid deficiencies, of which there are 21.

Ann is a great believer in Bach flower remedies, and once she has a diagnosis, she dowses her checklist to find which is the best remedy for any given illness or condition. From the most expensive race horses to the lowliest mongrel, Ann loves them all.

Experiences of a Master Dowser with George Applegate – Saturday 25th June 2011

They came from Cam and they came from Cornwall, Cheshire, Kent, and all points in between, to hear the 90-year-old master dowser, George Applegate. And he did not disappoint. With hardly a wrinkle to be seen, and a distinct sparkle in his eye, George delighted his audience of over 40 on June 25th.

During a lengthy career, which George claims to be 60 years but we suspect is far more, George has dowsed for 2,534 boreholes to be drilled throughout the world. The deepest so far was 2 miles, but he has just signed a contract for one even deeper at two-and-a-quarter miles. The widest was a metre across, a major undertaking.

George does not do the drilling himself, of course, but he masterminds each project, gets the permits and planning permissions, appoints the driller, decides where to drill, and all the other major considerations in between. A 100m high rig will carry rods that weigh 90 tons. "All my responsibility!" says George.

He has dowsed for Madonna. "I told her to stand close to me while I explained it." He has dowsed for Elton John, "but I told him to stand over there." He has even dowsed for Prince Charles, who needless to say had to have a go himself. "But he wasn't very good at it," murmured George.

George has a greater than 99.9 per cent success rate, but modestly chose to talk about a couple of rare failures. "Because, ladies and gentlemen," he said, "you don't learn from your successes, you learn from your difficulties and failures."

He must have learned a lot from one spectacular failure in Australia, where they had spent around £7M on drilling but hit a deep layer of rock that turned out to be impenetrable, and had never been discovered before. They brought in drillers from Texas at a cost of £5,000 a day, to no avail. The Australian Minister for Mines told George, "You found it, you better name it," so he called it Rotex. "Fortunately it wasn't my £7M," says George, "but I didn't get my fee either."

George then mentioned another failure, drilling back home at Bournemouth Golf Club through several layers of chalk and sand, until they reached strata comprising such fine sand it was almost like talcum powder. It was so fine it was simply backfilling the borehole. George suggested putting a steel tube down but still it invaded. There was water there, but it turned out to be dirty and unusable, so that project had to be written off.

His reputation remains unsullied, however, and he is famous in Australia. The scale of farms there is significantly larger than here. "A million acres of farm land," says George, "with 70,000 cattle. It had been very dry for over three years, no grass, cattle dying, so I had nine boreholes drilled for them. That worked, and I was treated like royalty."

Again in Australia, a group of farmers near Perth wanted him to come straight away, they were in desperate straits too. George told them I can't get a flight that soon, but they said leave the flight to us and sent him a First Class ticket. "I decided I liked champagne after my fourth glass," reports George, "and when the young lady attendant came along and offered me a pair of pyjamas to put on, I thought things were definitely looking up!"

One of George's major achievements is discovering how to dowse the geology of an area. It is important for a water diviner and his driller to know what strata they will be drilling through – limestone, sand, clay, chalk, etc., and even geological maps don't give enough detail. It has taken him six years to develop this ability, but tells us we'll have to wait for his next book before learning how it's done.

Another major achievement, of course, is his book,

The Complete Book of Dowsing: The Definitive Guide to Finding Underground Water.

"I wrote that so that the knowledge won't die with me," says George cheerfully. "Read Chapter 3," he recommends. "If you read that and understand it, you will have some useful information."

He leads you to believe there is another book on the way, but when pinned down, admits it might be some four years away. "So I'll have to live that long to write it." Losing his wife to cancer of the spine, which then spread, just a few years ago was a sad loss and, one senses, not least because of the amount of work she contributed towards his books.

But most important of all, George has achieved the love and respect of everyone with whom he comes in contact, and that's not just other dowsers and celebrities, but most government departments including coal boards, the MoD, Leyhill Prison, Wormwood Scrubs, British Rail, several hospitals, Severn Trent Water, RAF stations, the projected Stonehenge by-pass, the police, and not forgetting Billy Butlin who had a holiday camp full of unhappy campers because there was no water. The holiday camp king had a full rig standing by, collected George in his helicopter, and whisked him off to Minehead to dowse for water.

Everyone was concerned that, being so near the beach, the water would be salty and not potable, but George discovered excellent fresh water coming under the Bristol channel. It still produces a million gallons per day, and that was 60 years ago! He has since dowsed all Sir Billy's holiday camps.

He is always in hot demand so was mildly surprised one day when someone wanting an appointment in Milford Haven said, "I can't be here that day, I'm having tea with Aunty." George gently suggested his time and his dowsing were more important than tea with Aunty, but on this occasion, Aunty turned out to be the Queen!

During a lively question and answer session, someone asked how he had got started in dowsing, and discovered he could do it. "Mr Mullins," said George. "My father was a big contractor working on a large estate. His driller had drilled three holes, all dry, and somehow they found Mr Mullins, a dowser from Bath."

"We watched him do it. He dowsed with a hazel twig, and decided to drill right between two of the existing dry holes. We felt a bit sorry for him really, but then suddenly there was plenty of water, and everyone was pleased. So I got myself a hazel twig and discovered I could do it too. I had a bicycle – I was too young for a motorcycle at that time – and I used to cycle over to Mr Mullins in Bath, who took me on as his only pupil. We couldn't tell how deep the water was at that time, but we could definitely find it."

"If water is five miles away," says George, "I can go straight to it." He does not map dowse, and feels it is not accurate enough. And he always keeps in mind the catchment area for the rainfall. Usually 28 per cent of rainfall penetrates; a third runs off, a third evaporates.

"If the catchment area is impervious, for example, clay, 90 per cent of the rainfall will run off."

Asked if he ever resorted to primary water, ancient water to be found under the earth's crust, he said the oldest thing he had ever found was a piece of rock that was dated to be four thousand million years old.

"I have found water that was 5–6,000 years old, and I have tasted water that is 1,000 years old."

Further questions got George on to the subject of sidebands, an inevitable hazard when drilling. Any flow of water will send up sidebands either side of the main stream. Further out you then get another set of sidebands, and further out again you get another, three bands altogether.

George said in passing that angle rods weren't very good for finding out what depth the water is to be found. He uses his hands, his head, plastic/nylon style rods, his mind, in fact, his whole body.

He speaks cheerfully of his few failures, but on one occasion he was almost too successful. He had dowsed the best site for a borehole for a couple in Wool, Dorset, and the driller came to drill while George happened to be away working in Australia.

One morning he received an anguished phone call saying, "We've drilled where you said to drill. The water is spurting 22 feet in the air, we're getting 16,000 gallons per hour. What do we do to stop her?"

All he could advise over the crackling line to Australia was to cut a section from a tree branch, hammer it into the hole and use it as a cork.

They won't forget George Applegate in a hurry, and neither will we. It was a privilege to have him as our speaker.

Local Farmer in need of dowsing help
Thursday 7th July 2011

A local farmer in need of dowsing help is an irresistible plea to us dowsers. Rob Jewell of St Augustines Farm at Arlingham had just received his latest water bill and it was massive compared to last year's. This suggested he had a leak from his water pipes, which is at best annoying and at worst, expensive.

St Augustines has been in Rob's family for some 200 years. It is a delightful place, open to visitors and schools so that children can visit real countryside and see live calves, pigs and piglets, pygmy goats, chickens and miniature Shetland ponies. However, they all have to be fed and watered, and Rob's new water bill was eye-watering to say the least.

Slimbridge Dowsing Group to the rescue! We mustered the troops and seven of us descended on Rob's farm, rods at the ready.

Once we had established where the meter was, and that the reading was showing excessive flow in the pipe leading to the fields, we followed the route indicated by our dowsing rods across the meadows, over ditches, through stinging nettles (good for butterflies), into the pig pen (the natives were friendly), and beyond. The water pipes travel some distance, in order to reach the various animals in their pens and pasture.

Initially we asked for the flow of water per minute at various places along the length of the pipes. At first we were getting 1.8 gallons per minute, but further along the pipeline this dropped to 1.3 and at one point it was down to 0.8, which more or less confirmed our suspicions of a leak – but where?

This week's rain ruled out looking for a damp patch. Nearby ditches would have absorbed any overflow anyway. But gradually we worked our way along the pipe and eventually we believe we found what we were looking for.

"Please show me where there is a leak?" one lady asked of her rods, and they soon crossed. Then another lady, followed by a third gentleman, which seemed pretty conclusive to us. We asked whether the leak was at a join in the pipework – No. How much was being lost through the leak? About 0.5 gallons per minute, which is a regular drip, drip, drip, and mounts up rapidly.

We plan to return with a spade as soon as possible and do some digging. It will be rewarding to get a result and prove whether we were right or wrong.

Practical Dowsing Training with Peter Golding Saturday 23rd July 2011

If you see someone behaving strangely in your local supermarket, don't panic, it's probably one of us.

During Peter Golding's talk on Practical Dowsing Training on Saturday 23rd July, we learned that dowsing can be useful for finding out whether certain foods or products are good for us (or not). Using either a pendulum or even just dangling an arm and seeing which way it swings, can give us valuable clues.

Everyone can dowse, says Peter, in fact, it's difficult to avoid doing it – our body's receptors are on permanent red alert, and pick up all sorts of information all the time.

If you've ever said you felt something with every fibre of your being, you weren't far wrong. Peter quoted author Elizabeth Brown's book, *Dowsing*, which claims recent scientific research indicates that the key is in the micro-structures and fibres of each and every cell, not just in the brain but in the entire body.

So what we pick up on with our own personal communication equipment (called receptors) is the energy of everything else. The experts call this electromagnetic or quantum fields, but that's just energy to you and me. And since we all have these receptors, and we're all picking up on this stuff all the time, that explains why we're all interconnected.

After reassuring us that dowsing truly is just a matter of practice and confidence, Peter took us outside to find a water pipe between the village hall and the road, and then an electric cable. Knowing such utilities are usually buried underground, we all concentrated hard, formed a line and were delighted when everyone's rods crossed at the same time. "Now look up," instructed Peter, and there above us was the electricity cable in question!

After that we crossed the road to the churchyard and into the Glebe field (with the farmer's permission) to find the route of the underground sewer outlet pipe from the rectory next door, the outline of a long lost stable building, and for a group hug in our favourite energy spiral in the far corner of the field, which is always there and always uplifting.

Perceiving Auras and Aura Diagnosis with Dr Helen Ford – Thursday 11th August 2011

You know those old religious paintings where all the good guys get to wear a halo? And you've seen those tall pointed head-dresses called mitres worn by bishops of the high church? And you must have noticed that kings and queens always wear a crown made of gold, studded with massively precious stones, on state occasions.

Well, according to our speaker on Thursday 11th August, Dr Helen Ford, they are all to do with the aura, the energy field surrounding every living thing – people, animals and plants.

The halo was simply the outpouring of purest love from a deeply holy person. For those who can see auras, it surrounds the entire body, but around the head it appears to form a pointed cone, so the Bishop's mitre was a physical symbol of that, and shows his authority.

Gold is still used today for healing and as a homeopathic medicine, so wearing a gold crown was to help the king or queen feel pure love. The jewels are thought to instil trust.

Seeing auras is more difficult than we thought. Helen stood in front of a white screen, and instructed us to look at her but then through her, rather like de-focusing the eyes to see the shapes in those magic 3D pictures.

"Oh, ye-es," we said, "sort of." Some of us got it; most of us didn't, but didn't like to say so. Those of us that could see it at first, lost the ability after a while, and wondered if it was too demanding to maintain such intense concentration for so long?

Even if we can't see someone's aura, we can easily pick up on their energy. You take to some people immediately, others put your hackles up straight away. Where does that come from but their energy?

Having explained so much, Helen then gave us a demonstration of how colours can affect the aura, how it changes with the colours we wear and, even more importantly, how colours can affect how others perceive us.

Wearing red can make you feel strong, energetic, aware of your own sexuality and power, and even feel a clean and healthy anger. (Suppressed anger is not healthy).

Black is a closed colour, secretive, and shows defensiveness, a declaration that you are not going to allow anyone in, and equally you are not going to give anything out.

Pink emanates a loving warmth and tenderness. Helen says all mothers should wear pink! Orange says you are open to what comes, easy going and creative.

Wearing yellow will result in an increased aura because it conveys total self respect, whereas dark green can be hostile and unpleasant. Dirty colours feel polluted and suggest jealousy, sadness, impure energy. That said, emerald green is clear and bright, and says you are feeling loving, you are open-hearted and compassionate.

Blue too offers happiness and lightness of being, while purple, once thought to be the exclusive preserve of royalty and the church, makes you feel aligned and calm, in harmony with spirit and creation.

Grey declares you are a victim, the wearer's aura shrinks; we should not only avoid wearing grey, but also be wary of people wearing it.

We can even use our aura to create a buffer zone, our defence against attack and incoming bad energy. To align ourselves and create our own harmony, we simply need to honour ourselves, know what feels right, and remain assured in the face of what other people think. When we are aligned, the universe is looking after us, we can trust and feel relaxed and safe enough to put out pure love.

Index of Subjects and Speakers

Useful websites and e-mail addresses

Slimbridge Dowsing Group –
                        www.slimbridgedowsers.org.uk
British Society of Dowsers – www.britishdowsers.org
Ann Lodygowski – ann.annimel@gmail.com
Ced Jackson – www.FengShuiFutures.com
Diane Holliday, EFT – www.dianeholliday.co.uk
Dr Helen Ford – www.drhelenford.co.uk
Irenka Danielewicz-Herbert – ww.embodyforyou.com
Joey Korn – www.dowsers.com
Lightship Therapies – www.lightshiptherapies.net
Dr Patrick MacManaway – http://dragonlines.net
Maria Wheatley – www.theaveburyexperience.co.uk
Trish Mills – quicksilver7@btinternet.com
Peter Golding – www.petergolding.net or e-mail
                        mailto@petergolding.net